The English Language: A User's Guide

The English Language: A User's Guide

Jack Lynch
Rutgers University - Newark

For Lana

Table of Contents

Introduction

There's no shortage of writing manuals in print today—a whole sector of the publishing industry is devoted to grammars, handbooks, style guides, and *vade mecums* for students and business writers. Some are slim pamphlets that fit in a pocket; others are weighty tomes that take two hands to carry. Some offer supportive hand-holding for novices; others are curmudgeonly jeremiads against creeping barbarism. Classics of the genre have been in print for half a century, and new books appear every year. Why add another one to the pile?

I've written this little book because I hope it offers three things that aren't found in most other writing guides. The first has to do with the scope of the coverage: I include entries because (1) real people want advice on these topics, and (2) it's possible to offer useful advice on them in a paragraph or two. If a topic doesn't fit both criteria, I don't bother with it here. I could have produced a much longer guide, covering hundreds of other topics, but many questions have never come up in all the years I've been teaching writing. Other problems are common, but are almost impossible to discuss in a guide like this: on matters like the sequence of tenses or verbal parallelism, I could write page after page without helping anyone. (Besides, readers who know enough to look in a guide for "sequence of tenses" don't need this guide.) So I've limited my advice to topics that actually challenge real writers, and that can be addressed briefly.

The second reason for this book has to do with its tone and style. Too many guides are written—no, I take that back; *written* is too grand a word—too many guides are *compiled* by committees, no doubt on sound pedagogical principles and guided by the best-practices thinking of some organization or other. And textbook purchasers tend to favor the safe choices; books that never offend and never challenge their readers are the ones that do well in the market. The results, though, are too often unreadable. There are honorable exceptions—writing guides I admire fill several shelves in my study—but there aren't enough of them, and they rarely end up in the right hands. A handbook made up of limp commonplaces rendered in flabby prose can't help being counterproductive, because it never shows that reading and writing can be enjoyable. Instead it teaches students to efface themselves from their writing, leaving no personal voice at all. I have no patience with that sort of thing, and it was my distaste for the blandness of so many other guides that led me to write this informal and playful handbook. I don't pretend every sentence in here is a gem, but at least I've tried to let a human voice come through. I hope the result is more readable than the pabulum served up by many other textbook writers.

The third thing I try to accomplish in this guide is the most important, but the hardest to describe: instead of making authoritative declarations on what's right and wrong, I want to help readers to make up their own minds about the difficult questions. For two decades I've been paid to correct other people's writing, and it's often a thankless job. It's never pleasant to tell people about their mistakes, and the task becomes much more complicated when there are no clearly accepted standards of *why* some mistakes are considered mistakes. When a math teacher marks something wrong on an algebra test or when a chemistry teacher says a student failed to balance a chemical equation, it's obvious what they mean. But writing doesn't work that way: linguistic wrongness comes in many varieties, and when I correct someone's prose I have to take all those varieties into consideration. Sometimes I fix unambiguous mistakes—garden-variety typos, straightforward errors of grammar, unambiguously wrong word choices. Sometimes I suggest that something is controversial—*hopefully*, say, or a singular *data*—and, while it's not necessarily *wrong*, many readers will be distracted by it. Sometimes I think a sentence is filled with padding, words like *basically* and *quite* that contribute nothing. Sometimes I note that the style is a little less formal than I think appropriate for the situation. And sometimes I simply think a good sentence could be better if we moved this word over there, or traded this word for that. In a typical paper I might make dozens of such corrections and suggestions, and I always want to explain *why* I make the changes I do. How, though, to indicate what each correction means? Margins are only so wide, and there's room for only so much scribbling.

Most writing guides do a lousy job of explaining *why*. They reduce everything to thumbs-up or thumbs-down, yea or nay, permitted or forbidden—with a great many things listed as forbidden-and-don't-you-dare-ask-why. To judge from some textbooks, you'd think an angel dies every time someone dangles a participle. Small wonder, then, that people come to treat grammar and usage as matters of superstition. But it's important to understand what these so-called "rules" mean, which ones are really rules and which ones are just tips. Until you know *why* to avoid the passive voice, or *why* to use (or avoid) the serial comma, you'll have a hard time putting the rules into action—they seem like a huge and arbitrary collection of thou-shalt-nots.

The result is this guide—a miscellany of grammatical rules and explanations, comments on style, and suggestions on usage, with comments on the status of most of the advice contained here. Nothing is carved in stone, and many comments are frankly matters of personal preference—feel free to psychoanalyze me by examining my particular hangups and *bêtes noires*. I've tried, though, to be clear about which entries are hard-and-fast rules, which ones are a matter of personal taste, and which ones fall in between. Rather than announcing what you're "allowed" to do, I want you to make informed decisions on your own, and I try to give the information you'll need to make the inevitable judgment calls. I've also tried to be frank about situations where there are no easy solutions—where every possible solution still poses some problem—rather than dogmatically asserting that one answer is the right one.

I said some entries are about my own personal taste—this guide is a personal document from top to bottom, written over the years without benefit (or hindrance) of committee or editorial board. Since many readers care about credentials, I suppose I should be clear up front: I'm not a linguist or a specialist in transformational grammar, nor am I trained in rhetoric and composition. On the other hand, I've spent a long time studying English literature, and have done a fair amount of research on the history of the language from the seventeenth century through the twenty-first. I've written and edited books, articles, and journals for both academic and popular audiences. I've also taught writing at the university level for almost a decade and a half; before that I worked for nearly as long as an editor in a big corporation. Whether this experience qualifies me to pontificate on the language is for others to decide. But I write not as an objective expert, nor as a tireless champion of correctness, but as a professional writer, a professional editor, and a professional teacher of writing eager to share some of the things I've learned over the course of my career.

Academic linguists are wary of "prescriptive" grammars like this, guides that set out standards of correct and incorrect usage. Prescriptivists often insist that correctness reigned in the good old days, whereas we've been on the road to hell ever since. Many ill-informed grammarians vociferate about things they barely understand, and try to enforce "rules" with no basis whatsoever. The letters-to-the-editor pages in newspapers are often filled by humorless cranks and scolds who wag fingers and lecture about the days of yore, when people spoke properly, unlike the semiliterate barbarians of today. Pish-tosh, say I—that's nonsense. Like the academic linguists, I reject any story about linguistic "decline," in which the twenty-first century speaks a decadent and degraded version of the language of some golden age. I don't lie awake at night worrying about the decline of proper English or the prospect that we're all heading to some linguistic hell. (In my grumpier moods, I'm convinced the whole world's going to hell—but then, I'm convinced the whole world's been going to hell since time out of mind. In my more sanguine moods, I wonder whether hell isn't such a bad place to be after all.)

In other words, I didn't write this guide to "protect the English language," whatever that means. The English language has done just fine without me for the first fifteen hundred years of its existence, and will no doubt continue to thrive long after I've gone. It will, of course, continue to change, and many of the things identified as troublesome in this guide will probably be perfectly acceptable, even in formal writing, in a few decades. Some purists are bothered by *hopefully* or the singular *data*, though their numbers are declining, and I suspect they'll have all but disappeared before long. The number of people who complain about sentence-ending prepositions is falling steadily, and I doubt anyone will care in a generation or two. The smart money says that the word *whom*, effectively dead in informal conversation, will eventually disappear even from formal English—and I'll be glad to see it go. This is all in the natural course of things, and it doesn't bother me in the least.

Why, then, did I write a traditional usage guide if I'm not worried about preserving the English language?—why have I written a prescriptive handbook if I distrust prescription? Because plenty of readers still *do* care about these things, and you won't win them over unless you write with them in mind. In other words, I hope in this book to make your writing more *effective* by drawing your attention to things that continue to bother some readers, for good reasons or for bad. I've tried to make suggestions on things that are likely to *work*—by which, as you'll see throughout this guide, I mean *have an effect on your audience.* In fact the entry called AUDIENCE is the heart of this book, along with a few other vitally important entries—RULES and PRESCRIPTIVE *VERSUS* DESCRIPTIVE GRAMMARS. The rest is just a set of footnotes on these entries. If you understand what it means to have an effect on an audience, and if you understand that real-world readers have all kinds of wacky notions about what makes for good writing, then all the other rules will begin to make sense.

The entries in the book are of several types. Some are focused articles, usually short, on specific points of usage: should you use *a lot* or *alot*?—is there a difference between *that* and *which*, *shall* and *will*, *flammable* and *inflammable*?—can you *grow the economy*?—when should you use a semicolon? And some entries are just brief explanations of terms in grammar: what's a *neologism*?— what's *aspect*, or *voice*, or the *subjunctive mood*? Most of these entries are matters of precedent rather than taste, and they're fairly uncontroversial. They're also intended for quick reference.

Other articles are more general, and usually longer. Some of them tell little stories about linguistic history: why does it matter that English combines words from different language families?— who gets to decide what's acceptable and what's not? (See LATINATE *VERSUS* GERMANIC DICTION and ACADEMIES.) Some of them offer advice on ways you can make your writing clearer, more forceful, and more graceful: how can you arrange the parts of a sentence for greatest emphasis?—which words run the risk of confusing or even offending readers? In these more general entries I start to move into more controversial territory, and sometimes offer personal opinions. These articles aren't always suited for quick reference, but they lend themselves to browsing and absorbing over time, and in the long run they're just as important as the rules. Really bad writing is rarely a matter of broken rules—editors can clean these up with a few pencil marks. It's more often the result of muddled thought. Bad writers consider long words more impressive than short ones, and use words like *usage* or *utilization* instead of *use* or *methodologies* instead of *methods* without knowing what they mean. They qualify everything with *It has been noted after careful consideration*, and the facts get buried under loads of useless words. They pay no attention to the literal sense of their words, and end up stringing stock phrases together without regard for meaning. They use clichés inappropriately and say the opposite of what they mean.

I originally assembled this guide for students in my own English classes, but it has grown over the years to have two main audiences. The first is students, whether advanced high schoolers or university students. The second is people who've finished school but could use a refresher course on the language, especially those who find themselves expected to write (or edit others' writing) in their jobs. Because my advice is aimed at beginners rather than linguists or professional writers, I've steered clear of as much linguistic and grammatical jargon as possible, and have given rough definitions of the technical terms that seem necessary. (I take the same approach as Joseph Priestley, who wrote one of the first modern English grammars in 1761: "*Technical terms*," he explained, "have neither been affected nor avoided: more than are here introduced were judged unnecessary to explain all the varieties that occur in the *English language*: they have not been wholly avoided, because they admit of easy definitions; the language of Grammar is observed to be aukward without them.") This has sometimes meant sacrificing precision for convenience. More sophisticated writers will see many points to quibble over, and professional linguists will be able to find all sorts of inadequacies. But those sophisticated writers and linguists don't need a guide like this; I'm simply trying to get the idea across to tyros. Every article on points of grammar—dangling participles, split infinitives—begins with a practical definition of the term, followed by some useful rules, and examples of good and bad writing. Sometimes there are suggestions on how to identify possible problems. The definitions and discussions are not exhaustive, just quick and dirty rules of thumb. If you need more detail, consider one of the books in the last section, "Additional Reading."

I've opted for simplicity in organizing this book. Some guides are divided into topical sections, but the subdivisions help only those readers who already know how to classify everything—which is rarely the case with beginning writers. Other guides are arranged progressively, with each chapter building on what came before, but I'm realistic enough to admit that no one—well, almost no one—will read this guide from cover to cover. (Surely you've got better things to do with your time.) So I've used plain old alphabetical order, putting the entries (or at least cross-references to them) where I suspect people are likely to look for them. This means that entries sometimes seem to jostle uncomfortably next to each other in a strange hodgepodge—a definition of grammatical *agreement* followed by a short dissertation on the history *ain't* followed by a description of the abbreviation *a.k.a.* followed by a tip to trim constructions like *all of*—but such mingling isn't necessarily a bad thing. Besides, mixing the general entries in with the more specific ones, rather than segregating them into an introduction, probably increases the chance readers will stumble across them.

The only exception to the alphabetical order is the appendix on citation. This is probably more important to students than to the rest of the world; most bankers and insurance underwriters will see little benefit in the section on how to cite scholarly monographs (though business writers should pay more attention to citation than they do). But students are a big part of the intended audience for this book, and citation is a big part of student writing, and I didn't want to force them to pay for a separate guide for information on citation. I include the basics on two common styles of citation here.

Some closing comments on what this guide is *not*. First, while I hope it's useful to some non-native speakers of English, it wasn't written with them in mind. When I say "trust your ear," for instance, I'm assuming that ear has been trained by at least a decade of hearing the English language. Learners of English as a second or foreign language have all sorts of questions I'm not prepared to answer. Neither is this a book about the writing *process*—I don't offer advice on outlines, rough drafts, revision, research methods, and so on. That's not because they're unimportant, but because this isn't the place. Despite the facetious title, this guide doesn't pretend to be a comprehensive guide to the language. I hope to inculcate the right attitudes toward the language, but I can't include an entry on every possible disputed topic. An old Greek proverb declares *mega biblion, mega kakon*—a big book is a big evil—and I've tried to keep that in mind, limiting the guide to topics that are useful to real writers. Readers of the on-line version of this guide have suggested many additions and revisions over the years, and I've been grateful for the feedback. But I haven't tried to incorporate into this guide everything that readers have asked about, because there's no end to the entries that I could add. The handbooks on my shelf include advice on *hatching* versus *hachure*, *parlay* versus *parley*, and *dare say* versus *daresay*; they offer long sections on the nominal relative and hundreds of places in which to use a comma. Entries like these may be useful to someone, but there's no way I could include every bit of advice that may be useful to someone somewhere at some time—eventually the guide would grow to the size of a dictionary. I'm not trying to take the place of dictionaries or systematic grammars. If I can get my readers to understand that writing is about having an effect on an audience, and that they always have to be conscious of the concerns of their audience, then my work is done.

Using This Guide

The entries are arranged alphabetically; when an entry discusses two related words (such as *affect* and *effect*), it's alphabetized under the first one. Cross-references are plentiful, and are indicated in the text with SMALL CAPITALS.

At the end of many of the entries are examples of good and bad usage. I've flagged the examples with nine labels, which fall into four pairs and one straggler. Here's how to read the labels:

Wrong and **Right**: Virtually all professional writers and editors will agree that one form is clearly inferior to the other, and most will identify it as a violation of the widely understood rules of English. Of course there are occasions when such errors may be useful—in dialogue, or when you're trying to sound informal—but the things labeled "wrong" should generally be avoided in formal writing.

Disputed and **Preferred**: The examples labeled "disputed" will bother many readers, who may consider them "wrong," though not everyone will agree. Things like HOPEFULLY and PREPOSITIONS AT THE END are the classic examples: many good readers and writers don't care about them at all, but a significant audience finds them objectionable, and they'll think less of you if you use them. I usually side with the traditionalists on these questions, and encourage you to avoid the disputed usages. You needn't follow my recommendations slavishly, but be aware that at least some readers will be put off by violations of the rules, and may hold it against you.

Informal and **Formal**: Some usages are perfectly acceptable in speech and even in informal writing, but are out of place in more formal contexts—which is usually what's called for in college writing and in the business world. I've tried to label some usages that may not be suitable in formal writing. Make the judgment call: if you're in a T-shirt-and-jeans sort of mood, there's nothing wrong with the informal version; if your audience expects jacket and tie, go with the more formal one.

Weak and **Strong**: These aren't matters of "right" and "wrong" at all, simply suggestions for making your writing clearer and more effective. The word *only*, for example, can legitimately go in many places in a sentence. Some positions, though, have more *oomph*, and you can make your writing more powerful if you place the word carefully. In the same manner, there's nothing illegal about putting *however* at the beginning of a sentence, but it often works better if you tuck it in the middle somewhere. The word *basically* usually contributes nothing to a sentence other than a few syllables. In these cases I've offered what I hope are helpful tips for making your writing more effective, but they're nothing more than judgment calls.

House Style: Finally there are the questions that are settled by what's called HOUSE STYLE. They can include things like serial COMMAS, spacing around DASHES, spellings of words like *catalogue* and *theatre*, and whether to indent the first line of a block quotation: things that aren't right or wrong, but merely conventional. If a professor or a boss has guidelines for these things, follow them; if not, just try to be consistent with yourself. And if you're writing for publication or any other kind of distribution, don't be surprised (or disappointed) if an editor changes some of your preferences.

I've sometimes had to make judgment calls: is *try and*, for instance, an example of "informal" usage, is it "disputed," or is it flat-out "wrong"? I don't pretend that I've answered every question to everyone's satisfaction. Still, I hope that the examples and the labels give you some idea what status these rules have. I want readers to come away from this guide able to make stylistic judgments on their own, rather than depending on an authority ruling some things acceptable and others forbidden.

Acknowledgments

Professional writers know that every book is the product of collaboration—the myth of the solitary author is just that—but this book is far more collaborative than most, certainly the most collaborative thing I've ever written. What began as a short collection of notes for a corporate office mutated into a list of tips for students in my classes at the University of Pennsylvania, where I was working on my Ph.D. in English. When, in 1994, I decided to save photocopying expenses by taking advantage of a newfangled thing called the World Wide Web, it began to attract an audience far beyond my classes—and soon I was getting more than a thousand readers a day, then more than ten thousand. Now it's not uncommon for it to get forty or fifty thousand hits a day, giving me hundreds of thousands, maybe even millions, of readers over the years. And thousands of those readers have taken the time to write and offer comments. Some have been supportive, others openly hostile. Some have castigated me as a reactionary throwback for insisting on long-forgotten and obsolete shibboleths, others have blasted me a permissive do-as-you-pleaser with no regard for traditional English—and sometimes on the very same entry. But they've all been valuable to me as evidence about which entries worked and which didn't. These readers raised questions, asked for clarifications, caught me in stupidities, and kept asking for new entries—and so the guide grew over the next decade and a half to its current size and scope. It's a rare treat for an author to get that sort of advice on a book that has not yet appeared in print, and I'm grateful to them all.

I don't know the names of most of those thousands, but I can thank a few people by name. Pat Bens and Suzanne Stuhlman provided the initial stimulus (and probably had no idea what they were responsible for creating). A long friendship with Paul Fussell showed me what good writing should look like. Carolyn Jacobson, Erik Simpson, and Dan White, all colleagues in my graduate program at the University of Pennsylvania, poked around early drafts of this guide and offered helpful advice and specific examples. The members of the alt.usage.english newsgroup, especially Mark Israel and Bob Cunningham, had plenty of things, both good and bad, to say about it. John Straus, a colleague at Rutgers University in Newark, has asked his students to read the guide and then to quiz me on it. And of course my own students at Penn and Rutgers, the ones for whom I wrote the thing in the first place, have given me insightful feedback. It's been a pleasure working with Ron Pullins and Kathleen Brophy at Focus Publishing, who suggested the old on-line guide might make a handy booklet, and I'm also exceedingly grateful to the readers they lined up—Kelly Malone, David Sonstroem, and A. Abby Knoblauch—who gave me valuable tips in translating the guide into the new medium.

Finally I have to express a debt to Lana Schwebel, one of the finest writers, best teachers, quickest wits, and dearest friends I've ever known. She taught me a great deal about writing, about teaching, and about how to use the language, and I've shamelessly filched many of her ideas in my own writing, here and elsewhere. Over nearly a decade and a half she helped me in more ways than I can tally, and it pains me that she's not around to read this book and tell me how to make it even better. All that's left is for me to dedicate it to her memory.

A *or* An.

Both are forms of the indefinite ARTICLE, but they're used in different places. Use *an* in place of *a* when it precedes a vowel *sound*, not just a vowel. That means it's *"an* honor" (the *h* is silent), but *"a* UFO" (because it's pronounced *yoo eff oh*).

Most of the confusion with *a* or *an* arises from ACRONYMS and other abbreviations: some people think it's wrong to use *an* in front of an abbreviation like "MRI" because *an* can only go before vowels. Not so: the *sound*, not the *letter*, is what matters. Because you pronounce it "em ar eye," it's *"an* MRI."

One other tricky case comes up from time to time: is it *"a* historic occasion" or *"an* historic occasion"? Some speakers favor the latter—more British than American speakers, but you'll find them in both places—using *an* on longish words (three or more syllables) beginning with *h*, where the first syllable isn't accented. They'd say, for instance, "a hístory textbook" (accent on the first syllable) but "an históric event." (Likewise "a hábit" but "an habítual offender," "a hýpothetical question" but "an hypóthesis.") Still, most guides prefer *a* before any *h* that's sounded: *"a* historic occasion," *"a* hysterical joke," *"a* habitual offender"—but *"an* honor" and *"an* hour" because those *h*'s aren't sounded. That's much more common in American style.

Examples:

Wrong: A honor
An horrible time
An united effort
A FBI report

Right: An honor
A horrible time
A united effort
An FBI report

House Style: A historic day *or* An historic day.

The Above, The Following.

Many kinds of writing, especially in business and law, routinely use lists. It's common to introduce the items those lists with *the following* and to refer back to them by *the above*. There's nothing wrong with that, but you can often make a sentence clearer and punchier with simple PRONOUNS: instead of *the above topics*, try *these topics*—the context makes your subject clear.

Absent.

Absent is perfectly acceptable as an ADJECTIVE ("He was *absent* three days last week"; "Everyone recognized her comment as an insult directed at her *absent* coworker"). And though it's uncommon these days, *absent* can also be a VERB meaning "to keep someone away," as in *Hamlet*'s "Absent thee from felicity awhile."

But *absent* as a PREPOSITION, meaning "without" or "in the absence of," is JARGON from the worlds of business and law: "Absent further information, we'll proceed as planned." It's been around for a long time, but do we really need another two-syllable way of saying *without*?

Abstraction.

See CONCRETE LANGUAGE and PRECISION.

Academies.

Some countries have official organizations to issue rules on linguistic matters: the Académie Française in France and the Accademia della Crusca in Italy are the most famous. NEOLOGISMS are among their biggest concerns. These academies are charged with keeping their languages "pure," and that often takes the form of keeping non-native vocabulary out of their dictionaries. Their largest job for the last hundred years or so has been resisting the incursion of English words into their languages.

They're mostly fighting losing battles. France's Académie fought long and hard against *le weekend*, preferring the native French *fin de semaine*. But most French speakers simply ignore the official ruling, and use the familiar English word. Other common French words include *le showbiz* and *les bluejeans*. The Accademia della Crusca has been a little more tolerant: the most recent supplement to the official Italian dictionary, for instance, includes "Millennium bug," derived "Dall'inglese *millennium* 'millennio' e *bug* 'insetto.'" Most of the academies, though, try to minimize the incursion of "foreign" words into their languages.

But here's something worth noting: *no English-speaking nation has an official academy.* The upshot? *There's no "official" standard of what's right or wrong in the English language.* (And bear in mind that English, though it's by far the most common language in America, isn't the "official" language of the USA, just a *de facto* standard.)

That doesn't stop plenty of people from issuing decrees; I'm not above it myself, though I hope people take seriously my repeated claims that I'm not trying to issue RULES but suggestions. In fact we're all making suggestions, whether we recognize that fact or not. The suggestions can be wise or foolish, the suggesters likewise—but no one is more "authorized" than anyone else to make them.

People regularly write to me asking about some widespread usage, wondering whether "the rules have changed" since they were in school. I confess I don't understand what the question means. English doesn't really have "rules" in the sense of "decrees handed down by an official body." The English language changes, as all languages do, but there's no committee that votes on what's right or wrong.

Does that mean anything goes? Of course not. Some things are (almost) universally recognized as inferior; more to the point, some SHIBBOLETHS will make you look stupid before some AUDIENCES. And personal TASTE is always a consideration. But there's no official rule-book, and that means there's no agreement on many questions. Is it "right" to say

"We want to GROW the economy"? Is *disconnect* a noun? Can you use IRONIC to refer to things that are merely coincidental? I hate 'em all, but—until the revolution comes, and I become Tyrant—I get only one vote. (Mind you, when that glorious day dawns, things are gonna change: anyone who uses the word LIFESTYLE will be sent to the copper mines, and those who say IRREGARDLESS will be summarily shot. Meanwhile, though, I just get to grind my teeth quietly.)

See AUDIENCE, PRESCRIPTIVE *VERSUS* DESCRIPTIVE GRAMMARS, and RULES.

ACCENTS.

English borrows many words from other languages, but not all of those languages use exactly the same alphabet—French in particular uses a number of accents and other diacritical marks (like the cedille, the little comma-thingie on ç). The question is what to do with them in English. The general tendency is that newly imported words keep their accents; as they grow more familiar, the accents often disappear—for a long time, for instance, English kept the circumflex on the *o* in the word *rôle*, but that now looks quaint. The usual pattern is for the foreign alphabets to morph into the familiar English alphabet.

The accents are often retained, though, if there's any danger of confusion with another word, or if the pronunciation might be confusing. Without the accents, for instance, *résumé* is hard to tell apart from *resume*. (For advice on whether or not you need *two* accents on that word, see RÉSUMÉ.) Diacritical marks—other than accents on vowels—usually stay: the tilde on *ñ*, for instance, is usually preserved in Spanish words imported into English.

ACCESS.

For a long time, the word *access* was strictly a noun—you could *have access to* something, but you couldn't *access* anything. Only in the early '60s did people begin using it as a transitive verb, originally in technical and computing contexts. Now it's increasingly used in any context where *have access to* is used.

All of which is to say it's a comparatively recent NEOLOGISM, and some traditionalists still find it grating. Bear it in mind.

ACRONYMS.

Among the less pleasant by-products of the late, unlamented twentieth century is the acronym. What began as a harmless attempt to shorten long names has turned into a mania for reducing every committee, gizmo, or plan to a would-be clever acronym. Resist the urge to create them by the dozen, especially when they don't do any useful work.

Some purists insist the word *acronym* should apply only to pronounceable combinations of letters: by this standard NASA and SCUBA are acronyms, but MRI and NFL aren't (some use the word "initialism" for these latter abbreviations). If you care to make the distinction, feel free, but most people will have no idea what you're talking about.

Note that acronyms are extremely rare before the twentieth century. If ever someone suggests an older word comes from the initials of some phrase—*posh* from "port out, starboard home," for instance—the story is probably bogus.

For tips on using *a* or *an* with acronyms, see A OR AN. See also PERIODS.

ACTION VERBS.

Action VERBS, as the name suggests, express *actions*; contrast them with verbs of *being*. Think of the difference between *I study* (action verb, even if it's not the most exciting action) and *I am a student* (verb of being).

Your writing often becomes livelier if you cut down on verbs of being, replacing them with action verbs. Contrast the clunky "She was the editor of a series of books" with the more direct "She edited a series of books."

Be careful, though, not to confuse action verbs with the active VOICE, which is the opposite of the PASSIVE VOICE. Sentences with verbs of being (such as *am, is, are, were*) aren't necessarily *passive* sentences, even if they're often weak ones.

See also E-PRIME.

Examples:

Weak: Hemingway was the writer of some of the most influential American novels of the twentieth century.
Her new book is a forceful expression of her views.
These are new visitors who have a lot to learn.

Strong: Hemingway wrote some of the most influential American novels of the twentieth century.
Her new book forcefully expresses her views.
These new visitors have a lot to learn.

ACTIVE VOICE.

See PASSIVE VOICE.

A.D., B.C., C.E., B.C.E.

All four abbreviations are used with years, but they have different CONNOTATIONS. It was a sixth-century monk, Dionysius Exiguus, who first thought of dating events since the birth of Jesus (though scholars say he got the date wrong by a few years). Eventually his system caught on in Christian Europe, and events were dated *A.D.: anno domini*, or "in the year of the Lord." Events that happened earlier were marked with *B.C.*, "before Christ." (Hard-core traditionalists put *B.C.* after the date, and *A.D.* before it: "44 B.C.," but "A.D. 1066.")

The system began in Europe and for a long time was used only in Christian cultures; the rest of the world used other systems. By the middle of the twentieth century, though, Dionysius's system of reckoning years after the birth of Jesus had become the norm throughout the world, at least for secular purposes. (Other systems, like A.H.—*anno hegirae*, "in the year of the hegira"—are still used in various religious traditions, but for secular business, Dionysius carried the day.) It makes life much easier not to have to convert: "When it was 1827 in America, what year was it in Turkey?" But, while the numbers are now the same the world over, it seems odd, and perhaps insensitive, to date events in the history of Islam, or medieval Japan, or pre-Columbian Mexico, with respect to the birth of Jesus, since these cultures either didn't know of Jesus at the time or don't consider him central to their belief.

As a way out, many writers use *C.E.* and *B.C.E.* (with or without the periods) for "common era" and "before the common era." This acknowledges that the once-Christian dating system has become the de facto standard—it's the "common era," shared by many societies—while respecting other cultures that may be uncomfortable expressing years before or after the birth of a figure who's not central to their belief system. You can use them if you choose; just be conscious of their effect on your AUDIENCE.

See also POLITICALLY LOADED LANGUAGE.

ADJECTIVES AND ADVERBS.

An *adjective* is a word that MODIFIES a NOUN or a PRONOUN: it answers *which one, how many*, or *what kind*. Some examples: "the *big* one"; "*seven* books"; "a *devoted* student." (Most adjectives can also go in the PREDICATE position after the verb: "This one is *big*;" "That student is *devoted*.")

Adverbs, on the other hand, usually modify verbs, and answer *in what manner, to what degree, when, how, how many times*, and so forth. Some examples: "He ran *quickly*"; "I'll do it *soon*"; "We went *twice*."

Sometimes adverbs modify not verbs but adjectives or other adverbs: "She finished *very* quickly" (*very* modifies the adverb *quickly*, which in turn modifies the verb *finished*); "The work was *clearly* inadequate" (*clearly* modifies the adjective *inadequate*, which in turn modifies *work*).

The easiest way to spot adverbs is to look for the telltale *-ly* suffix: *easily, quickly, quietly*, and so on. Be careful, though; not all adverbs end in *-ly*, and not all *-ly* words are adverbs. *Soon, twice*, and *never*, for instance, are adverbs (they tell when or how often); *friendly*, *ugly*, and *northerly* are adjectives (they modify nouns).

Some stylistic advice: go easy on the adjectives and adverbs. It would be foolish to cut them out altogether, but many people overuse them. Too many adjectives and adverbs tend to make your writing sound stilted or faux-poetic, and they rarely add much precision. Your nouns and verbs should be doing the hard work, with adjectives and adverbs playing only a supporting role. As Strunk and White put it, "The adjective hasn't been built that can pull a weak or inaccurate noun out of a tight place."

ADVISE.

"Please advise"—on its own, without, say, "Please advise me about the new rules"—is a verbal tic common among memo-writers. I find it ugly and inelegant, but I promise not to make too great a fuss as long as it's confined to business writing.

AFFECT *VERSUS* EFFECT.

An easily CONFUSED PAIR. *Affect* with an *a* is (usually) a VERB; *effect* with an *e* is (usually) a NOUN. When you *affect* something, you have an *effect* on it. The usual ADJECTIVE is *effective*, which means "having the right *effect*," or "getting the job done"—an *effective* medicine, for instance. (It can also mean "in effect," as in "the new policy is effective immediately.")

If the *usual*s leave you curious, here's the rest of the story: *affective* as an adjective means "relating to or arousing an emotional reaction"; *effect* as a verb means "to bring about" or "to accomplish," as in "to effect a change." There's also the noun *affect*, usually used in psychology, meaning "an emotion" or "feeling."

Examples:

Wrong:	The plan to increase the troops had the desired affect on the enemy.
	Caffeine usually has no affect on me.
	I didn't think such a little change would effect the outcome.

Right: The plan to increase the troops had the desired effect on the enemy.

Caffeine usually has no effect on me.

I didn't think such a little change would affect the outcome.

AFFIXES.

Affix is a technical term to describe bits stuck to (*affixed to*) root words. In English, we use mostly *prefixes* (*fore-*, *un-*, *pre-*, *anti-*) and *suffixes* (*-less*, *-ish*, *-ness*, *-ful*). Some languages have *infixes*, where parts are added to the middle of a root word, but they're rare in English outside of language games.

AFRICAN AMERICAN.

The long history of slavery and racism in America has made the choice of words to describe people of African descent especially sensitive. Words once used without malice can later become offensive. If you want to avoid giving offense to your readers, exercise some care.

American history is littered with abandoned terms. *Negro* was once common as both a noun and an adjective; ditto *colored* or *colored people*. In the 1960s, the compound *Afro-American* became common. Today they're all rarely used, having been edged out by *African American* (with or without the hyphen), which gained popularity in the 1980s. It has the advantage of being modeled on other terms for American ethnicities: Irish-American, Italian-American, and so on. (Among African Americans whose families have been in America for a long time, it's difficult to pinpoint a particular country of origin, so we're usually left with the name of the continent rather than the nation. Remember that we also use *Asian American*, so it has a parallel.)

Black is still probably the most common word for people of African descent. (Although people descended from Egyptians or white South Africans are technically "African American," the term is rarely used for anyone who's not black.) Some prefer to capitalize *Black*—"the Black community," for instance—though most guides prefer lowercase, especially if you use *white* in lowercase.

One last thought. You'd think it would be too obvious to need mentioning, but I've occasionally heard people refer to citizens of South Africa or Brazil or Great Britain as "African American." Erm—they're not American, so they can't be African American.

See POLITICALLY LOADED LANGUAGE.

AGGRAVATE.

The word *aggravate* traditionally means "to make worse." You can, for instance, aggravate a *problem*, *situation*, or *condition*: "The new medicine only aggravated my indigestion." (It comes from Latin, and originally means "make heavier": the *-grav-* in the middle is from the same root as *gravity*.) The more controversial question is whether you can aggravate a *person*. It's common to use the word in colloquial speech as a SYNONYM for *irritate*, *exasperate*, or *annoy*: "The salesman's attitude really aggravated me," for instance. It's probably wise, though, to tread carefully in more FORMAL settings, where some people find it inappropriate.

Examples:

Informal: The way he always finishes my sentences really aggravates me.

Formal: The way he always finishes my sentences really annoys me (or "*irritates* me").
The bad weather is only aggravating the situation.

AGREEMENT.

One of the fundamental RULES of GRAMMAR is that the parts of a sentence should *agree* with each other. It's easier to demonstrate than to define agreement.

Agreement is usually instinctive in native English speakers. In "I has a minute," the verb *has* doesn't agree with the subject *I*. We would say "I *have*." In "John got their briefcase," assuming John got his own briefcase, *their* should be *his*. It's obvious.

Only rarely does it get messy. A PLURAL noun right in front of the singular verb can throw you off. Consider "Any one of the articles are available": the verb *are* shouldn't agree with *articles*, but with the real subject of the clause, *one*: the sentence should read, "Any one of the articles *is* available."

A PREPOSITION or a verb that governs two PRONOUNS can also cause problems. In "He wanted you and I for the team," the word *I* should be *me*: he wanted *you* and he wanted *me*, so he wanted *you and me*. (HYPERCORRECTION is always a danger in cases like this. Pay special attention to phrases like *you and I, you and she*, and so forth.)

See also EACH, EVERY, DATA, MEDIA, PHENOMENA, and PLURAL.

AIN'T.

This paradigmatic example of "incorrect" usage provides a good opportunity to talk about what "incorrect" means.

A venerable bit of schoolyard wisdom advises that *"Ain't* ain't in the dictionary, so *ain't* ain't a word." There's only one problem with this pithy apothegm: it ain't true. Any DICTIONARY worth its salt should contain *ain't*—though it will probably also include some usage note pointing out that it's "nonstandard," "slang," "colloquial," or "informal."

Is *ain't* "a word"? Of course it is. The question is whether it's a *good* word, which always means an *appropriate* word. So how do you decide whether it's appropriate?

Ain't—like an earlier form, *an't*—is a contraction of *are not*, and is often used for *am not* or *is not*. It's been around since the eighteenth century (the *OED* records the first example of *an't* in 1706, and of *ain't* in 1778). That's the period that saw the birth of several of our common contractions, including *don't, won't*, and *can't*. So *ain't* has a long pedigree, it's a perfectly logical and consistent construction, and it's widespread.

Does that mean it's an appropriate word?—Well, yes and no. Yes in the sense that you can use *anything* if it's effective in context; no in the sense that, since the nineteenth century, many people have campaigned against it as vulgar and illiterate, and many continue to believe that. You have to bear that in mind when you write and speak, and you have to adjust your language to your AUDIENCE.

In many formal contexts, *ain't* will mark you as poorly educated: it's unwise, for instance, to use it in a job application. On the other hand, there are times when *ain't* gives exactly the sort of colloquial tone you're looking for. There's all the difference in the world between "You ain't seen nothin' yet" and "You've not yet seen anything."

The moral of this story: usages aren't "correct" or "incorrect" in any abstract sense; there's no logical way to puzzle out whether something is legitimate or not. You can't simply look in "the dictionary" to figure out whether something is a word. Every word carries its history with it. As always, it's entirely a matter of writing for your AUDIENCE—but if you've spent any time reading this guide, you know that already.

A.K.A.

An abbreviation for "also known as." It's usually printed as three lowercase letters with periods after each letter: *a.k.a.*

ALBEIT.

Albeit means "although," "but," or "even though," but it usually involves a different syntax. The word rarely introduces a CLAUSE because it contains its own verb, and can be interpreted as "although it should be" or something like that. In other words, "It was a hot day, albeit it was a dry one" is unidiomatic; you don't need that second verb, and can go with "It was a hot day, albeit a dry one."

If you're not confident about that, it's probably best to avoid the word and go with a garden-variety *but* or *although*. The word is fairly rare, and not often found outside FORMAL contexts and LEGAL WRITING.

ALL OF.

"All of the ——" can usually be rewritten as "All the ——,"
"All ——," or "Every ——." Strive for ECONOMY.

Examples:

Weak: All of the people in the office were evacuated.

Strong: All the people in the office were evacuated.
Every person in the office was evacuated.

ALOT.

Nope: *a lot*, two words. (That's *a lot* meaning *much, many,
often*, and so on. There's another word, the verb *allot*, which
means "to distribute or apportion"; but the adjectival or
adverbial phrase *a lot* is always two words.)

ALRIGHT.

Two words—*all right*—is preferred.

ALSO.

Avoid beginning sentences with *also*. There's nothing *illegal*
about it, but it tends to be inelegant. The suggestion is that
your writing is just a list, and this next item is merely an
afterthought. Much better is to find logical TRANSITIONS from
one sentence to the next.

Examples:

Weak: Also, you should read the small print before
signing the contract.

Strong: You should also read the small print before
signing the contract.

ALTERNATE *VERSUS* ALTERNATIVE.

Alternate (as an ADJECTIVE) traditionally means going back
and forth between two things, as in *alternate Mondays* (i.e.,
every other Monday). *Alternative* means *other*. There's not much
risk of confusion, but it can't hurt to be precise. Traditionalists
prefer an *alternative* to an *alternate* plan. (*Real* traditionalists

insist that *alternative* can be used only in cases where there are two options.)

Examples:

Disputed: He made an alternate suggestion.

Preferred: He made an alternative suggestion.

A.M., P.M.

Whether it should be *a.m.*, *am*, *A.M.*, or *AM* (and the same with *p.m.*)—that is, whether it should get capital letters and whether it should get periods—is a matter of HOUSE STYLE. The lowercase version without periods (*am*, *pm*) is probably best avoided, since *am* is already a word, and there's a risk of confusion. The others are all acceptable.

What about noon and midnight? The abbreviations stand for *ante meridiem* and *post meridiem*, "before noon" and "after noon." Technically, then, noon is neither a.m. nor p.m., even though many clocks treat noon as 12:00 p.m. Better is to spell out "noon" or "midnight" to eliminate any prospect of confusion.

AMERICA.

Some object to the use of *America* when you mean *the United States of America*, because, after all, the Americas constitute an entire hemisphere containing dozens of nations—Suriname and Guyana are in the Americas, too. The problem is that, while we can use the noun phrase "United States," we don't have a corresponding adjective, and there's really nothing other than "American" to describe things related to the U.S. Besides, the proper name of Mexico is Estados Unidos Mexicanos ("the United Mexican States"), so even "United States" isn't as precise as we'd like.

So—be aware that some readers may dislike *America* to stand for just one part of the Americas, but know that there aren't many good solutions.

P.S.: I hope I don't have to explain that the adjective *American*, even when it's limited to the citizens or inhabitants of the United States of America, doesn't mean "white" or "of European descent." The United States has been a multi-ethnic society since the very beginning. *American* is a national, and not an ethnic, designation, so you should never contrast *American* with, say, *Jewish* or *Arab*.

AMONG *VERSUS* BETWEEN.

Some guides say you should use *between* for two things, and *among* for more than two. Not everyone agrees, but you'll rarely go wrong if you follow this guideline.

Examples:

Disputed: The money was divided between all the members of the band.

Preferred: The money was divided among all the members of the band.

AMOUNT.

The word *amount* refers only to *mass nouns*, not to *count nouns*: it's an *amount of stuff* but a *number of things*. In other words, it's wrong to refer to "the amount of students in the class" or "the amount of songs on my iPod": you mean "the *number* of students in the class" or "the *number* of songs on my iPod."

See COUNT *VERSUS* MASS NOUNS and FEWER *VERSUS* LESS.

Examples:

Wrong: There's a ridiculous amount of papers in that class.

Right: There's a ridiculous amount of homework in that class.
There's a ridiculous number of papers in that class.

AMPERSAND.

Ampersand is the name for the & symbol (in all its different forms). It began life in ancient Rome as a scribal shorthand for the Latin word *et*, and in some typefaces you can still spot the original *e* and *t* in the symbol. Today it's used in the names of many corporations, publishers, and law firms ("Dewey, Cheatem & Howe," or Thomas Pynchon's brilliant "Salitieri, Poore, Nash, De Brutus & Short"), as well as in some trademarks (M&M's). When you refer to firms or products like this, preserve the ampersand that's the official part of their name. Ditto if there are ampersands in any material you're quoting: QUOTATIONS should always be precise. But don't use the ampersand in your own FORMAL WRITING where the word *and* is expected.

AND AT THE BEGINNING.

See BUT AT THE BEGINNING.

AND/OR.

And/or is sometimes mandated in LEGAL documents, but just clutters other writing. One word or the other will almost always do just as well; if you need to be really precise, you can spell it out as "A, or B, or both." See SLASHES.

ANTECEDENT.

Antecedent—pronounced *ant-uh-SEE-dent*—is a technical term in GRAMMAR for the word or phrase to which a relative PRONOUN refers. In a sentence like "She couldn't stand opera, which always sounded like shrieking," the relative pronoun *which* stands in for the word *opera*, so *opera* is the antecedent. In a sentence like "He couldn't say the word *titillate* without giggling, which always got him in trouble," the word *which* refers back not to any individual word, but to the whole preceding clause ("He couldn't say the word *titillate* without giggling")—the whole thing is the antecedent.

A common fault in writing is to leave the antecedent in a sentence or clause unclear. Especially when sentences begin with the word *This*, readers may be baffled about the subject. If you think your audience might be confused, be explicit.

ANTICIPATE.

For traditionalists, to *anticipate* something is to get ready for it, or to do something in advance; this isn't the same as *expect*. If you *expect* changes, you think they'll be coming soon; if you *anticipate* changes, you're preparing to deal with them. William Blake certainly didn't *expect* Modernist poetry, but in some ways he *anticipated* it by doing similar things a century earlier.

The use of *anticipate* for *expect* is now so widespread that it's pointless to rail against it. Still, *expect* has the advantage of being shorter and more to the point. Don't give in to the business writer's love affair with the LONGER WORD.

ANXIOUS *VERSUS* EAGER.

I prefer to avoid using *anxious* when I mean *eager*. *Anxious* is related to the word *anxiety*; it traditionally means "worried, uneasy." It's often used, though, where *eager* or *keen* would be more appropriate. You can be anxious about an upcoming exam, but you probably shouldn't tell friends you're anxious to see them this weekend. It's not that it's *wrong*, but it runs the risk of confusion.

ANYMORE *VERSUS* ANY MORE.

The one-word version means "these days" or "since then," as in "We don't do it that way anymore." The two-word version is used for other senses: "We don't have any more coffee." Keep them straight.

ANY WAY, SHAPE, OR FORM.

Feh. Not only a CLICHÉ, and therefore bad enough in its own right, but an uncommonly *dumb* cliché. Will someone please tell me what's wrong with "in any way"?

APOSTROPHE.

The most common way to form a POSSESSIVE in English is with apostrophe and *s*: "a hard day's night." After a PLURAL noun ending in *s*, put just an apostrophe: "two hours' work" (i.e., "the work of two hours"). If a plural doesn't end in *s*—*children, men, people*—plain old apostrophe-*s*: "children's," "men's," "people's." It's never "mens'" or "childrens'."

There's also the opposite case: when a singular noun ends in *s*. That's a little more complicated. Most style guides prefer *s's*: *James's house*. Plain old *s*-apostrophe (as in *James' house*) is common in JOURNALISM, but most other publishers prefer *James's*. It's a matter of HOUSE STYLE.

Note that the possessive PRONOUNS *hers*, *its*, and *theirs* never take an apostrophe.

Apostrophes are sometimes used to make acronyms or other abbreviations PLURAL (another matter of a local HOUSE STYLE). My preference: don't use apostrophes to make abbreviations plural—not "She learned her ABC's," but "She learned her ABCs." The only exception is when having no apostrophe might be confusing: "Two As" is ambiguous (it might be read as the word *as*); make it "Two A's." Don't use apostrophes as SINGLE QUOTATION MARKS to set off words or phrases (unless you need a quotation within a quotation).

Using an apostrophe to refer to a decade—the *1960's* versus the *1960s*—is another matter of house style; again, journalists tend to use the apostrophe, and most other publishers don't. I prefer to omit it: refer to the *1960s* or the *'60s* (the apostrophe indicates that "19" has been omitted), not the *1960's* or (worse) the *'60's*.

See also MICROSOFT WORD for tips on distinguishing *apostrophes* from *single quotation marks*.

APPARATUS.

The *-us* at the end suggests to many people that the PLURAL should be *apparati*, but it's not. *Apparatus* is a Latin noun, but it doesn't belong to the group that takes a plural in *-i*. The original Latin plural is simply *apparatus*, same as the singular.

You can use that in English, or you can make it a regular plural with *apparatuses*. See also CORPUS, GENIUS, GENUS, OPUS, and VIRUS.

APPOSITION.

Two phrases are in *apposition* when they're logically equivalent and in the same grammatical relation to the rest of the sentence: it's a way of explaining a word or phrase, or giving additional information about it. It's easier to see in examples than in definitions.

Consider the sentence "I spent the year in my favorite city, Detroit." It puts two phrases—"my favorite city" and "Detroit"—in apposition; the second phrase explains the first. Or "I just finished a novel by D. H. Lawrence, the least talented novelist in English"—the phrase "the least talented novelist in English" is in apposition to "D. H. Lawrence," and gives the writer's opinion of Lawrence. (It happens to be correct, by the way—you heard it here first.)

Apposition usually requires COMMAS around the appositional phrase: "The winter of '24, the coldest on record, was followed by a warm summer." They're sometimes omitted when a proper name follows some sort of relation: "My brother Bill works in electronics," for instance. In most such cases you can safely go either way, though many writers prefer to use the commas when they're describing a unique relationship: "My husband Phil came from Pittsburgh," for example, may suggest to some readers that the writer has multiple husbands, and this is just clearing up which one, whereas "My husband, Phil, came from Pittsburgh" leaves no doubt.

Oh, yeah—don't confuse *apposition* with *opposition*. They come from the same Latin root (*pono* 'put'), but have nothing else to do with one another.

ARTICLES.

English has two sorts of *articles*: the *definite article* (*the*), and *indefinite articles* (*a* and *an*). They function more or less as ADJECTIVES. The USAGE of definite and indefinite articles is one of the hardest things for speakers of other languages to master, because it's often entirely arbitrary—why are you *in town* but *in the village* or *in the city*? And BRITISH usage sometimes differs from American usage; wounded Brits end up *in hospital*, while Yanks are *in the hospital*. I'm afraid I have no easy rules that are even a little helpful—all I can suggest is that non-native speakers pay close attention to the actual usage of articles. Sorry.

As *versus* Like.

In FORMAL WRITING, avoid using *like* as a CONJUNCTION. In other words, something can be *like* something else (there it's a PREPOSITION), but avoid "It tastes good *like* a cigarette should"—it should be "*as* a cigarette should." Quickie test: there should be no VERB in the phrase right after *like*. Even in phrases such as "It looks like it's going to rain" or "It sounds like the motor's broken," *as if* (or *as though*) is usually more appropriate than *like*—again, at least in FORMAL WRITING.

Examples:

Disputed: It seemed like it was never going to end.
            She went at it like there was no tomorrow.
            Like I said earlier…
            He acted like he was a movie star.

Preferred: It seemed as if it was never going to end.
            She went at it as if there was no tomorrow.
            As I said earlier…
            He acted as if he was a movie star
                or
            He acted like a movie star.

Assure, Ensure, Insure.

While *ensure* and *insure* aren't quite so clear cut, *assure* is very different from both. You *assure a person* that things will go right by making him confident. Avoid using *assure* in the sense of "Assure that the wording is correct"; you can only *assure somebody* that it's correct.

Ensure and *insure* are often used interchangeably, but I like to keep them separate. *Insuring* is the business of an insurance company, i.e., setting aside resources in case of a loss. *Ensure* means *make sure*, as in "Ensure that this is done by Monday."

British writers, by the way—and for all I know, other Commonwealthers—sometimes use *assurance* where Americans use *insurance* (it's life *assurance*, but auto *insurance*, in the UK). But it's not for me to pass laws with Transatlantic jurisdictions.

Examples:

Wrong: Assure your bring your ticket with you.

Right: Ensure you bring your ticket with you.
or
Make sure you bring your ticket with you.

As to Whether.

Plain old *whether* often does all you need to do. See ECONOMY and WASTED WORDS.

As Far As.

You need a verb: "As far as such-and-such *goes*," "As far as such-and-such *is concerned*." Plain old "As far as such-and-such," widespread though it may be, is frowned upon.

Examples:

Disputed: As far as money, she was really happy with her new job.

Preferred: As far as money goes, she was really happy with her new job.
or
As far as money is concerned, she was really happy with her new job.

ASPECT.

Aspect is a property of VERBS that's a little tricky to describe. Here's how the *American Heritage Dictionary* defines it:

> A category of the verb denoting primarily the relation of the action to the passage of time, especially in reference to completion, duration, or repetition.

Okay—what does that mean? Whereas TENSE describes whether an action happened in the past, present, or future, *aspect* indicates whether it happened once, happens all the time without stopping, happens intermittently, or is happening now. Some languages (especially Slavic ones) indicate aspect in their verb forms; in English, we do most of it with AUXILIARY VERBS or adverbs. Consider the differences between these:

I go to class.

I'm going to class.

I went to class.

I was going to class.

I have gone to class.

I had gone to class.

I have been going to class.

I had been going to class.

I will go to class.

I will have gone to class.

And so on. Linguists use the word *perfect* to describe a completed action and *imperfect* to describe one that is (or was) incomplete; they also use *progressive* or *continuous* to indicate whether an action is ongoing. Some also have a category for whether action is *habitual*. And different languages handle these things differently. English doesn't have many different verb forms for these things, but we can indicate all sorts of differences with our AUXILIARY VERBS; when that's not clear enough, an adverb can resolve ambiguities.

AS YET.

Consider using *yet*. See WASTED WORDS.

Asyndeton and Polysyndeton.

These two big, scary Greek words have to do with the placement of the word *and*.

A list usually takes the form of "A, B, C, and D" (with or without the final COMMA, which is a matter of HOUSE STYLE): in other words, commas to separate the items, with the CONJUNCTION *and* before the last item. There are times, though, when it's appropriate to depart from the usual rule.

Asyndeton means "not bound together"; it refers to cases when you leave out the conjunction *and* altogether: "A, B, C, D." It can create a greater sense of speed, of motion: think of Julius Caesar's famous declaration, "I came, I saw, I conquered." *Polysyndeton* means "extra bound together"; it refers to cases when you use the conjunction *and* after each item: "A, and B, and C, and D." It often produces a more formal and stately tone, a measured consideration of each item. The English translation of the Hebrew Bible (the Old Testament) includes many examples of polysyndeton.

Use things like this sparingly. An occasional departure from the normal rule can be striking and can really improve the rhythm or flow of your prose, but if you do it all the time it becomes an annoying verbal tic.

At This Point, At the Present Time, At This Point in Time.

Why? You don't need them—*now* is clearer and more direct, and *so far* covers most of the other possibilities. See CURRENTLY and WASTED WORDS.

Audience.

The key to all good writing is *understanding your audience*. Every time you use language, you engage in a *rhetorical* activity, and your attention should always be on the effect it will have on your audience.

Some people become very defensive about their language, and bristle when someone has other preferences. Especially with POLITICALLY LOADED LANGUAGE, but even with things as trivial as SPLIT INFINITIVES, they think that readers are upset for silly reasons, and that they shouldn't be forced to change their usage. They're adamant that their audience *shouldn't* be upset by such things, and they resent the way other people's irrational prejudices are supposed to shape their own language. Remember, though, that it's not all about you. It's about your audience, and that audience will have all sorts of concerns that you may not share. You don't get to choose those concerns; you simply have to learn to work with them.

Think of GRAMMAR and STYLE as analogous to, say, table manners. Grammatical "RULES" have no absolute, independent existence; there's no Grammar Corps to track you down for using "whose" when "of which" is more proper, just as Miss Manners employs no shock troops to execute people who eat their salads with fish forks. You can argue, of course, that the other fork works just as well (or even better), but both the fork and the usage are entirely arbitrary and conventional. Your job as a writer is to have certain effects on your readers, readers who are continuously judging you, consciously or unconsciously. If you want to have the greatest effect, you'll adjust your style to suit the audience, however arbitrary its expectations.

A better analogue might be clothing. A college English paper or a document in a business office usually calls for the rough equivalent of the jacket and tie (ladies, you're on your own here)—a little dressier than you'd wear at home, but not a suit, and certainly not a tuxedo. However useless or ridiculous the tie may be, however outdated its practical value as a garment, certain social situations demand it, and if you go into a job interview wearing a T-shirt and jeans, you only hurt yourself by arguing that the necktie has no sartorial validity. Your job is to figure out what your audience expects. Likewise, if your audience wants you to avoid ending your sentences with PREPOSITIONS, no amount of argument over historical validity will help.

But just as you shouldn't go under-dressed to a job interview, you shouldn't over-dress either. A white tie and tails will make you look ridiculous at a barbecue, and a pedantic insistence on grammatical BUGBEARS will only lessen your audience's respect for you. There are occasions when *ain't* is more suitable than *is not*, and the careful writer will take the time to discover which is the more appropriate.

Usually your goal is to keep as many of your readers happy as you can. All readers have their hangups and pet peeves, and will be distracted if you use words or phrases they dislike; that distraction means you're less likely to get what you want. There are significant numbers of readers, for instance, who get upset over SPLIT INFINITIVES, PREPOSITIONS AT THE END of sentences, and the word HOPEFULLY, so it's often in your interest to avoid them. Then again, you may want to be in-your-face and irritate some of your readers. That's fine, as long as it's a conscious decision: if you've done the mental calculation and have concluded that you can afford to alienate part of your audience, knock yourself out. There are times when it's rhetorically effective to irritate one faction in order to please another. Just be sure you're always aware of the effect you're having on your audience.

Of course you can never hope to keep *every* reader satisfied— some people have weird obsessions. Over the years I've received plenty of messages from cranks with downright bizarre notions of what's right and wrong. If you don't put your prepositions at the end of sentences, you may run into readers who think you should. If you work to avoid SEXIST LANGUAGE so as not to offend one class of readers, you may end up irritating the traditionalists who view gender-neutral language as politically correct pandering. But you can play the odds, and work to keep *most* readers on your side, or at least the ones you're most eager to please.

If you're writing for a school assignment, of course, your audience usually consists of exactly one person, your teacher or professor. But everything in this entry still applies. Your instructor's job is to stand in for a more general audience; he or she should try to avoid any personal hangups and respond to your writing the way a more general audience will. (No one does it perfectly; professors are only human—most of them, anyway—and can't always transcend their own limitations. But they're supposed to try.) So, even when your *real* audience consists of a single reader, you should still imagine a larger audience, one made up of educated but nonspecialist readers. This way you get to practice on one person before you're let loose on the larger reading public.

See DICTION, FORMAL WRITING, PRESCRIPTIVE *VERSUS* DESCRIPTIVE GRAMMARS, RULES, SHIBBOLETHS, and TASTE.

AUXILIARY VERBS.

Some highly INFLECTED languages can express a whole range of VOICES, MOODS, or ASPECTS by modifying the form of the main verb. English, though, doesn't have many forms of each word, so we depend on *auxiliary verbs*, also called *helping verbs*, to express these things. They include *be* (in all its various forms, like *is*, *was*, and *will*), *have* (ditto), *can*, *might*, *may*, *must*, *should*, *could*, *would*, and *ought*. There's also the so-called "dummy auxiliary" *do* (along with *did*), which is used for emphasis, for forming negatives or questions, and for changing tense.

These auxiliary verbs differ in usage from other verbs. First, most of them don't change form in the third-PERSON singular: while you say "I walk, he walks," it's "I can, he can" or "I would, he would"—there's no *cans* or *woulds*. (The exceptions are *be*, *have*, and *do*, which become *is*, *has*, and *does* in the third-person singular.) Second, you form the negatives by putting *not* (or *never*) *after* these auxiliary verbs: "do not worry," "it may not happen," "she has not answered," "you could not have known." Third, you can form questions by reversing the order of the subject and the auxiliary verb: "will you be home?"

See also USED TO.

Back-Formation.

Sometimes a root word looks to the untrained eye like a combination of a root and one or more "affixes"—that is, prefixes or suffixes. For instance, some nouns ending in -*ar*, -*er*, or -*or* seem to be made up of a verb with a suffix on the end: *burglar*, for example, seems to mean "one who *burgles*," and *scavenger* seems to come from *scavenge*. Historically, though, it's the other way around: the "simple" or "root" forms are actually derived from the longer words. There's also the word *peas*, which seems to be the plural of *pea*—the original word was *pease* (as in the old nursery rhyme, "pease-porridge hot"), a mass noun, and only later did people assume that if you could have *pease*, you must be able to have a *pea*. People looked at the word *sleazy* and thought the *y* at the end was turning the noun *sleaze* into an adjective—the way *frosty* comes from *frost* or *wealthy* comes from *wealth*—but there was no noun *sleaze* until after there was an adjective *sleazy*.

The resulting words are called *back-formations*. Here's a list of common ones, far from complete: *accrete* (from *accretion*), *destruct* (from *destruction*), *diagnose* (from *diagnosis*), *edit* (from *editor*), *emote* (from *emotion*), *enthuse* (from *enthusiasm*), *escalate* (from *escalator*), *flab* (from *flabby*), *funk* (from *funky*), *injure* (from *injury*), *intuit* (from *intuition*), *kidnap* (from *kidnapper*), *orate* (from *oration*), *peddle* (from *peddler*), *televise* (from *television*), and *tweeze* (from *tweezers*).

These back-formations aren't necessarily *wrong*; most of those above are now part of Standard English. And of course some can be used for comic effect: you might say someone is *gruntled*, for instance, or *ept*, or *chalant*.

But when they're new, they'll strike many people as odd. Liaise, for instance—which seems to be the root of the noun *liaison*—is actually derived from it; and in America, at least, it's still struggling for acceptance. Be careful.

BACKSLASH.

See SLASHES.

BASICALLY.

Almost always useless. Qualifiers such as *basically, essentially, totally,* and so on rarely add anything to a sentence; they're the written equivalent of "Um," and too often take the place of real intellectual engagement. In my years of teaching I've read many thousands of sentences containing the word *basically,* but I can't remember a single one that was necessary. See WASTED WORDS, and read it twice.

BASIS.

See ON A —— BASIS.

BEGGING THE QUESTION.

It doesn't mean what you think it means. *Begging the question*—from the Latin *petitio principii*—is a logical fallacy; it means assuming your conclusion in the course of your argument. If you say "Everything in the Bible must be true, because it's the word of God," you're taking your conclusion for granted. If you say "The defendant must be guilty because he's a criminal," you're doing the same. It's a kind of circular logic. The conclusion may be true or false, but you can't prove something by assuming it's true.

This is very different from *raising the question,* though people are increasingly using the phrase that way. It's sloppy, and should be avoided. Here, for instance, is a piece from *The Times (London),* 30 Nov. 2004:

> The behaviour of ministers is a matter for prime ministers, who appoint and dismiss them. But this begs the question of who should find out what has gone wrong on behalf of a prime minister.

No it doesn't. It *raises* the question; it *prompts* the question; perhaps it *forces* us to ask the question; maybe this question *begs for an answer.* But it doesn't *beg the question.* If you mean *it makes me wonder,* say *it makes me wonder.*

BEHALF.

Traditionalists observe a distinction between *in behalf of* and *on behalf of.* The former means "for the benefit of": you might write a letter of recommendation *in behalf of* a colleague, or raise money *in behalf of* hurricane victims. The latter means "on the part of" or "as the agent of": a lawyer acts *on behalf of* her client, or the producer may accept an award *on behalf of* the cast.

BEING THAT.

An overused and inelegant idiom, favored by those who want to sound more impressive. It probably comes from "it being the case that," maybe with some influence from "given that" and "seeing that," but it doesn't make much sense. (*Being as* has the same problems.) Avoid it. Use *because, since,* or something similarly direct.

Examples:

Disputed: Being that we missed the last train, we spent the night in the city.

Preferred: Because we missed the last train, we spent the night in the city.

BETWEEN YOU AND I.

Between you and I?—*Between you and I?*—Tsk, tsk, tsk. It's between you and *me.*

First, the technical explanation: *between* is a PREPOSITION; it should govern the "objective case." (In English, that's a concern only with the PRONOUNS.) A preposition can't govern a pronoun in the subjective (or nominative) case, even when there are multiple pronouns after the preposition.

That explanation should be enough for the serious grammar nerds. For the rest of you, think of it this way: when you have two pronouns after a preposition, try mentally placing each one directly after the preposition. "Between you" should sound right to your ear, but "between I" jars: "between *me*" sounds much more natural. Since it's "between you" and it's "between me," it should be "between you and me."

Ditto other prepositions, like *for, to, from, with, by*, and so on. If something is for her and also for me, it's "for her and me," not "for she and I"; if Akhbar gave something to him and also to them, he gave it "to him and them," not "to he and they." Try putting the preposition directly before all the following pronouns, and then use the form that sounds right in each case.

The problem probably arises from HYPERCORRECTION: it sometimes seems that *you and I* is "more correct" than *you and me*. It's not—at least, it's not always. Be careful.

BIMONTHLY (BIWEEKLY, BIANNUAL, BIENNIAL).

Many people are confused: does *bimonthly* mean "every two months" or "two times a month"? It turns out that they're confused for a good reason: the word means both things. (Ditto *biweekly*, which can mean "every two weeks" or "twice a week," and *biannual* or *biennial*, which can mean "every two years" or "twice a year.")

Some purists insist *bimonthly* means every other month, and use *semimonthly* (or *biweekly*, which is nearly the same thing) to mean twice a month. Eminently rational—but *bimonthly* has had both meanings practically since the beginning, so there's not much historical support for the policy. Worse still, even if you decide to adopt this distinction, you can't rely on your audience to be familiar with it.

What to do? When you're writing, your safest bet is probably just to abandon the words *biannual, biennial, bimonthly*, and *biweekly* in any context where you're not certain your audience will understand what you mean. When you're reading, be aware that there are several possibilities, and be careful not to make vacation plans based on an event that may not be happening.

It's not a very elegant solution—it always seems a pity to lose a word—but your first obligation is always to be understood.

BLACK *VERSUS* AFRICAN AMERICAN.

See AFRICAN AMERICAN.

BLOCK QUOTATIONS.

Short QUOTATIONS usually appear in the text surrounded by quotation marks, "like this." Longer direct quotations, though—and sometimes shorter quotations of poetry—should be set off as *block quotations* or *extracts*, thus:

> Notice that the quotation is indented on both sides: most word processors make that easy. Notice, too, that you *don't* use quotation marks around a block quotation: the indention is enough to indicate it's a quotation. Some HOUSE STYLES prefer block quotations to be single-spaced, others like them double-spaced; check to see what your readers expect.

How long is long?—practice varies. Many publishers suggest fifty words as the cut-off—shorter than fifty, run in the text; longer than fifty, indented extract—though others use a hundred words as a guideline. Poetry is more often set off in indented extracts, since it makes the line breaks clear without resorting to slashes.

Always be sure to include proper citations in block quotations; the usual route is to put either a footnote reference or the citation in parentheses *after* the closing punctuation in the quotation itself.

BLUNTNESS.

Bad writing is often wimpy writing. Don't be afraid to be blunt. Consider things like "There appear to be indications that the product heretofore referred to may be lacking substantial qualitative consummation, suggesting it may be incommensurate with the standards previously established by this department": what's wrong with "It doesn't work"? Of course you should be sensitive to your reader's feelings—there's no need to be vicious or crude, and saying "It sucks" won't win you many friends—but don't go too far in the opposite direction. Call 'em as you see 'em, and have no truck with weasel-words and mealy-mouthed EUPHEMISMS.

BOLDFACE.

There's no reason to use boldface in typescript; spend your time writing, not fiddling with the word processor. See FONTS, ITALICS, and TITLES.

BRACKETS.

See INTERPOLATION.

BRITAIN.

Americans are often unaware of the cluster of nations and ethnicities hiding under words like *Britain*, *British*, and so on. This isn't the place for a long lecture on the history of the cluster of islands off the northwest coast of Europe, but a quick tour might save Yanks the embarrassment of getting something grossly wrong.

The biggest island, the one to the east, is called Great Britain; it contains three significant chunks: England, the biggest part; Wales, to the west; and Scotland, to the north. In the Middle Ages, England, Scotland, and Wales were all separate nations, often warring, that happened to share an island. In 1536, Wales became an English principality and ceased to have its own government and its own legal system. Scotland shared a king with England beginning in 1603, and officially became part of Great Britain in 1707, again having its government folded into the Parliament in London. The Welsh and the Scots had their own cultural and ethnic identities, but their government had become part of the larger British Parliament.

The next biggest island, to the west of Great Britain, is Ireland, which contains two nations. The bigger part, to the south, is the Republic of Ireland; though long under British rule, it's been an independent nation since 1922, and can no longer be described as British. The smaller part is Northern Ireland, and that's still governed from London. Put it together with Britain and you get the United Kingdom of Great Britain and Northern Ireland.

That cluster of islands is traditionally called the British Islands (or British Isles) and, though the Republic of Ireland isn't happy about it, there doesn't seem to be a better choice.

These topics have become especially POLITICALLY LOADED in recent years, as Scottish and Welsh nationalism has been on the rise, and the Scots and the Welsh are eager to distinguish themselves from the English. In 1997—for the first time in centuries—Scotland and Wales got their own parliaments. England, Scotland, and Wales are still part of Britain; their inhabitants can be called Britons; the adjective is British. But they're also English, Scottish, and Welsh, and those terms aren't interchangeable. You can see it if you travel around Britain today. Thirty years ago you'd see the British flag, the Union Jack, all over the place. Now it's much more common to see the flags of England, Scotland, and Wales.

Unless you're writing specifically about the internal politics of the British Isles, you needn't worry about all the complicated history and national dynamics. Still, you should know that it's a potential political minefield. You'll generate a lot of ill will north of the River Tweed if you refer to Sean Connery, for instance, as an English actor. He's British, but he's Scottish, not English. Roddy Doyle, the Irish novelist, writes in English, but he's not English himself, neither is he British. Tread carefully.

BRITISH SPELLINGS.

Although the large majority of words are spelled the same way around the English-speaking world, there are some small differences between British and American English. (Of course other English-speaking countries have their own rules, which usually look to me like a medley of British and American spellings.) Many words that end in -*ize* in American English are often spelled with -*ise* in British English (*sympathize, sympathise*); many words that end in *-or* in America end in *-our* in Britain (*honor, honour*); many consonants that are single before suffixes in America are doubled in Britain (*traveled, travelled*). A good DICTIONARY will show you most of the differences.

If you do use British spellings, use them consistently. Inconsistent British spellings are an affectation. A few words can legitimately go either way: both *theater* and *theatre* are acceptable in America, likewise *catalog* and *catalogue*; both *analyze* and *analyse* are used in Britain. But dropping in the occasional *colour* into American writing is a bad idea.

See also -ISE AND -IZE.

BUGBEARS.

Arguments over grammar and style are often as fierce as those over Windows versus Mac, and as fruitless as Coke versus Pepsi or boxers versus briefs. Pedantic and vicious debates over knotty matters such as PREPOSITIONS AT THE END, THAT VERSUS WHICH, and SPLIT INFINITIVES may be entertaining to those who enjoy cockfights, but do little to improve writing. Know as much as you can about the RULES, but strive above all for CLARITY and GRACE. Think always of the effect you'll have on your AUDIENCE. Over time you'll come to trust your ear, which will be disciplined by reading the best authors and by constant practice at writing. See also PRESCRIPTIVE VERSUS DESCRIPTIVE GRAMMARS, RULES, and TASTE.

BUT AT THE BEGINNING.

Contrary to what your high school English teacher may have told you, there's no reason not to begin a sentence with *but* or *and*; in fact, these words often make a sentence more forceful and even GRACEFUL. They're often better than beginning with *however* or *additionally*. Beginning with *but* or *and* often makes your writing less FORMAL;—but worse things could happen to most writing than becoming less formal.

Note, though, that if you open with *but* or *and*, you usually don't need a COMMA: not "But, we did it anyway"; it's enough to say "But we did it anyway." The only time you need a comma after a sentence-opening conjunction is when you want to sneak a clause right between the conjunction and the rest of the sentence: "But, as you know, we did it anyway."

One other thought: avoid beginning several sentences in a row with *but*. It gives the impression of a tennis match, with your attention going from one side to the other and back again.

Can *versus* May.

Traditionalists often insist on this RULE, but few writers adhere to it strictly. Still, if you can do it gracefully, use *can* to refer to possibility, and *may* to refer to permission.

Cannot.

Always one word, even in FORMAL contexts where you don't see many other CONTRACTIONS. Note, though, that *could not* is still two words, unless you use the contraction *couldn't*.

Examples:

Wrong: You can not imagine how hot it is here.
Right: You cannot imagine how hot it is here.

Can't Help But.

The *can't help but* construction (with other forms of the verb, like *cannot* and *could not*) is a little illogical: it seems to come from two other constructions, *can't help —ing* (meaning "I can't keep myself from —ing") and *can't but* (meaning "I can't do anything except"). So *can't help but* should mean "I can't keep myself from doing anything except," a kind of double negative. Still, *can't help but* has been around for a long time (the *OED* traces it to 1894), and it's probably not going away, so it's not worth grousing about. I avoid it myself, preferring "can't help —ing," and you should know it distracts some readers, but there are more important things to worry about.

Examples:

Disputed: I can't help but wonder how he did it.
Preferred: I can't help wondering how he did it.

Cant *versus* Can't.

Both are real words, and your SPELLING CHECKER won't be able to tell you which is which. The more common word is *can't* with an apostrophe; it's a contraction of *cannot*. Much rarer is *cant* without an apostrophe: it has a lot of meanings, including "empty speech," "thieves' slang," "jargon," "hypocritical piety," and so on.

See also WONT *VERSUS* WON'T.

CAPABLE.

The phrase *is capable of——ing* can usually be better rendered as *is able to ——*, or even turned into an active VERB with *can ——*. See WASTED WORDS.

Examples:

Weak: The new machine is capable of printing twenty pages a minute.

Strong: The new machine is able to print twenty pages a minute

or

The new machine can print twenty pages a minute.

CAPITALIZATION.

It's customary to capitalize:

The first word of a sentence;

The first word in a line of poetry;

The major words in the TITLE of a work;

Proper nouns (names), including some ADJECTIVES derived from proper nouns (*Spanish* from *Spain*, *Freudian* from *Freud*);

Personal titles when they come before a name (Mr. Smith, Ms. Jones, Dr. X, Captain Beefheart, Reverend Gary Davis, Grand Vizier Lynch);

All (or several) letters in an abbreviation (NASA, MRI, SoHo).

There are a few exceptions. Some acronyms have become so common that we've nearly forgotten their origins, and treat them as common words: radar (radio detecting and ranging), scuba (self-contained underwater breathing apparatus), laser (light amplification by stimulated emission of radiation).

It's sometimes difficult to figure out what counts as a proper noun: it's customary to capitalize *Renaissance* and *Romantic* when they refer to historical periods, but not when they mean any old rebirth or something related to romance. (Even more confusing, the noun *Middle Ages* is usually capitalized, but the adjective *medieval* isn't, even though they refer to the same thing, and one is just a Latin translation of the other. Go figure.)

It's common to capitalize President when referring to *one* President of the United States, but you'd refer to all the presidents (no cap) of the U.S., and the presidents of corporations don't warrant caps unless you're using president as a title. Go figure.

In some HOUSE STYLES, the first word of an independent clause after a colon gets a cap: "It leads us to one conclusion: Not enough bands use horn sections." I don't much like it, but *de stilis domorum non est disputandum*—there's no arguing about house styles.

One other note: DON'T USE ALL CAPITALS FOR EMPHASIS. It makes your writing look amateurish, and it's more difficult to read. (Mixed upper- and lowercase is easier to read, since the eye recognizes the overall shape of the words, with their ascenders and descenders. ALL CAPS simply appear as blocks, and readers have to slow down to figure them out.)

See EMPHASIS, HOUSE STYLES, and TITLES.

CASES.

English has comparatively few *cases*, for which you should get down on your knees and thank the good Lord above.

Cases are alterations in the forms of NOUNS and other SUBSTANTIVES, sometimes along with their MODIFIERS, that show the grammatical function they play in a sentence. In other words, in some languages nouns assume different forms depending on whether they're the subject of a clause, the DIRECT OBJECT, the indirect object, or relationships like ownership, place, motion, and so on.

In ancient Greek and modern German, nouns and pronouns can take four cases: nominative, genitive, dative, and accusative. In Latin, you have those four, plus ablative. Finnish has boatloads of cases: nominative, genitive, accusative, partitive, inessive, elative, illative, adessive, ablative, allative, essive, translative, instructive, and abessive (I'm probably missing a few). As you get further from the Indo-European languages, you get ever more exotic cases: the Kalaallisut language of Greenland, for instance, has ten cases, absolutive, ergative, equative, instrumental, locative, allative, ablative, perlative, nominative, and accusative.

When English was more heavily INFLECTED in the OLD ENGLISH period, there was a considerable set of cases. Today, though, nouns take only two cases, one for the POSSESSIVE (usually with apostrophe *s*), and one for everything else. Our PRONOUNS are still inflected differently for the *subjective* and the *objective* cases (*subjective* being a term some people use for the *nominative* case).

It's clearest in some examples. Take the singular noun *friend*. Whether it's a subject, a direct object, or an indirect object, it stays the same; it changes only to show possession: "My *friend* lives nearby" (subject); "I called my *friend*" (direct object); "She gave my *friend* a call" (indirect object); "I forgot my *friend's* address" (possessive).

Pronouns, on the other hand, take different forms: "*He* lives nearby" (subject); "I called *him*" (direct object); "She gave *him* a call" (indirect object); "I forgot *his* address" (possessive). Here the personal pronoun *he* has one form when it's a subject, another when it's an object (whether direct or indirect), and yet another when it's possessive.

Native speakers almost never have any trouble with this: only rarely do they use the subjective case when the objective is called for, as in "He gave it to you and I"—*I* should be *me*, since it's the object of the verb *gave*. See the entry for AGREEMENT.

CENTER AROUND.

Center on is better than *center around*. One thing can *revolve around* another, but the center is a point; you should therefore *center on* something.

CENTRALIZED.

Use *central* whenever possible; the *-ized* ending rarely contributes anything but an extra syllable. See PERSONALIZED.

-CENTURY.

The rule for HYPHENATING compounds like *twentieth century*: if the phrase is used as a NOUN, no hyphen; if it's used as an ADJECTIVE, hyphenate it. So: "It was one of the greatest disasters of the twentieth century," but "It was one of the greatest twentieth-century disasters." (Since *twenty-first* is already hyphenated, you refer to *twenty-first-century disasters*.) That's the general rule for compound phrases: hyphenate them when they're used as adjectives. See also COMPOUND WORDS.

Examples:

Wrong:	The new plan helps the middle-class.
	The new plan helps middle class workers.
Right:	The new plan helps the middle class.
	but
	The new plan helps middle-class workers.

CF.

Cf. is an abbreviation of the LATIN word *confer*, which means "compare." It's often used in footnotes and other citations— something like "Cf. p. 227" or "Cf. *Tom Sawyer*, chap. 2"—to say "Compare the passage I've just discussed with another one." It's not exactly the same as "see also," but it's similar. Note that it's an abbreviation of a single word, so there's just one period at the end.

CLARITY.

Along with GRACE, one of the paramount writer's virtues. Your job is to make yourself clear to your reader. Let nothing get in the way. Many of the entries in this guide—especially AUDIENCE, PRECISION, OBFUSCATION, and VOCABULARY— address clarity.

CLAUSES.

See DEPENDENT *VERSUS* INDEPENDENT CLAUSES.

CLEARLY, OBVIOUSLY, UNDOUBTEDLY.

My English professor instincts kick in—my Spidey-Sense starts tingling—whenever I see these words. Too often they're used when something is unclear and doubtful, but the author simply doesn't know how to make the point convincingly. Clumsy writers want to make an argument but don't know how to bridge some conceptual gap. Instead of painstakingly working out the logic, they simply state their conclusion with an *obviously* (when it's not at all obvious). When I see such words, I immediately suspect the writer is fudging something complicated.

There's nothing inherently wrong with the words, but be sure to use them honestly.

CLICHÉS.

"Avoid clichés" is such common advice that it's almost a cliché itself, but no worse for that. It's stated especially clearly by Thomas Pinney in his *Short Handbook and Style Sheet*:

> [Clichés] offer prefabricated phrasing that may be used without effort on your part. They are thus used at the expense of both individuality and precision, since you can't say just what you mean in the mechanical response of a cliché.

George Orwell's advice is overstated for effect, but it's still good to bear it in mind: "Never use a metaphor, simile, or other figure of speech which you are used to seeing in print." If you're depending on a stock phrase, you're letting someone else do half your thinking for you.

A comprehensive catalogue of clichés is beyond me, but here's a list of the more egregious ones that get under my skin (with cross-references to those that get their own entries elsewhere in the guide):

> absolutely;
>
> ANY WAY, SHAPE, OR FORM;
>
> at the end of the day;
>
> the blame game;
>
> FEEL (for *think*, *believe*, etc.);
>
> hot-button issue;
>
> MASSIVE or massively;
>
> playing the race card;
>
> sending a message;
>
> SOLUTION;
>
> 99% for anything just shy of complete (sometimes with even more significant digits, as in 99.999%); 110% effort.

They're not clever, they're not funny, they're not memorable, they're not convincing. They're prefab strips of language, hastily tacked together, and they do you no good.

If you *must* resort to clichés, though, be especially careful not to muddle them. Remember, for example, that the more widely accepted phrase is "I *couldn't* care less," not *could*: the idea is that "It would be impossible to care about this subject any less than I already do." And a U.S. senator, trying to reassure his constituents that the budget talks were going well in spite of the apparent chaos, told reporters, "It's always darkest before the *storm*," rather than "before the *dawn*"—he thereby unintentionally suggested that things are going to get worse, not better. Pay attention to every word.

Don't confuse these mangled clichés with MIXED METAPHORS—though a mixed metaphor *might* result from a botched cliché, they're not the same thing.

Neither should you confuse clichés in general with IDIOMS, the natural way to say something. The desire to avoid clichés shouldn't make your language oddball. Learning to tell the difference between the two is an important skill, and one you can develop only over time.

CLIMACTIC *VERSUS* CLIMATIC.

Climactic with the extra *c* comes from the word *climax*, and refers to a high point. *Climatic* without the extra *c* comes from the word *climate*, and refers to the weather. Don't confuse them.

COLONS.

A *colon* marks a pause for explanation, expansion, enumeration, or elaboration. Use a colon to introduce a list: thing one, thing two, and thing three. Use it to pause and explain: this sentence makes the point. Use it to give an example: this, for instance.

There are other uses. The section on citation at the end of this guide includes tips on colons in bibliographies. Americans use it after the salutation in a formal letter: "Dear Sir:" (the British generally use a comma, which we Americans restrict to less formal letters). It also often introduces a BLOCK QUOTATION or a list of bullet points.

See also SEMICOLON (don't confuse them!) and the end of CAPITALIZATION.

COMMAS.

A complete guide to comma usage is beyond the scope of a guide like this, but I can offer a few tips. I'll start with a few places commas should be *avoided*:

After the CONJUNCTIONS *and*, *but*, and *or*, unless the comma sets off a phrase that can't stand alone as a sentence. It's wrong to write "But, she did get it done on time." Use the comma only if there's such a phrase, as in, "But, *to be fair*, she did get it done on time." See also DEPENDENT *VERSUS* INDEPENDENT CLAUSES.

Between a month and year in a date: not *November, 1990*, but *November 1990*. The comma stops two sets of numerals from running into one another, as in *November 20, 1990*.

Some style guides call for omitting the comma after very short prepositional phrases at the beginning of a sentence: not "On Saturday, the office is closed," but "On Saturday the office is closed." But *do* use a comma after long prepositional phrases or dependent clauses: "*Because the entire epic is concerned with justifying the ways of God to man*, Milton must present free will in a positive light." (How many words do you need before "short" turns into "long"?—trust your judgment, and think always about clarity.)

For the usage of commas in large numbers, see NUMBERS.

Finally, the thorniest comma-related question, whether or not to include the *serial comma* (also known as the *Oxford comma* or *Harvard comma* from its inclusion in their house style guides). In most house styles, the comma is preferred before the last item in a list: "the first, second, and third chapters." Leaving it out—"the first, second and third chapters"—is common in JOURNALISM, but usually not recommended for other kinds of writing. While it saves a teensy bit of space and effort, omitting the final comma runs the risk of suggesting the last two items (in the example above, the second and third chapters) are some sort of special pair. A famous (and probably apocryphal) book dedication makes the danger clear: "To my parents, Ayn Rand and God."

Oh, yeah—go and read the entry on SEMICOLONS for good measure.

COMMA SPLICE.

A *comma splice* is probably the most widespread variety of RUN-ON SENTENCE: it's where two independent clauses are stuck together with just a comma. You usually need some better way to attach them to one another: use a period or a semicolon in place of the comma; use a coordinating conjunction like *and* or *or*; or use a subordinating conjunction like *because* or *although*.

Cc The English Language: A User's Guide

Examples:

Wrong: My iPod broke, I haven't listened to music in a week.

Right: My iPod broke; I haven't listened to music in a week.
or
My iPod broke, so I haven't listened to music in a week.
or
Because my iPod broke, I haven't listened to music in a week.

COMMUNITY.

The word *community* gets a real workout in a lot of modern political writing—the black community, the Latino community, the gay community, and so on. I know it's very widely used, and I'm fighting a losing battle, but I don't much like the term. It suggests to me a degree of coherence that can be found in very few populations. I won't grouse too much if you use it, but I don't have to like it.

See POLITICALLY LOADED LANGUAGE.

COMPARATIVES.

The comparative is the form of an adjective or adverb that implies a greater degree than the "positive" (base) form of the word: not *good* (positive) but *better* (comparative); not *hot* (positive) but *hotter* (comparative); not *arbitrary* (positive) but *more arbitrary* (comparative). The next step up is the *superlative*: not *good* or *better* but *best*; not *hot* or *hotter* but *hottest*; not *arbitrary* or *more arbitrary* but *most arbitrary*.

As the examples suggest, there are three basic ways to form comparatives. A few are irregular: *good, better, best; bad, worse, worst; far, farther, farthest; little, less, least.* These simply have to be memorized, although virtually all native speakers learn them in early childhood. (Young children might say *gooder* and *goodest*, but they pick up on the irregular forms quickly.)

Most adjectives form their comparatives with *-er* (sometimes doubling the final consonant, sometimes turning a final *y* into *i*, and if the word ends in *e*, adding simply the *r*): *slower, bigger,* *happier, wiser.* The superlative of these adjectives is formed with *-est*: *slowest, biggest, happiest, wisest.*

But a large class doesn't take *-er*; it's formed with *more*: not *arbitrarier* but *more arbitrary*; not *exhausteder* but *more exhausted.* (The superlatives of these adjectives is formed with *most*: *most arbitrary, most exhausted.*)

You can't always say for sure which class an adjective belongs to. Short adjectives—one syllable—usually take the *-er* form. Long adjectives—three or more syllables—take *more* rather than *-er*: you'd never say *condescendinger* or *unaccountabler.* But the two-syllable adjectives can go either way. A good DICTIONARY will give you the comparative and superlative form of most adjectives; if ever you're in doubt, look it up.

COMPLEMENT *VERSUS* COMPLIMENT.

To *complement* something (with an *e*) is to complete it or make it up to a whole; to *compliment* something (with an *i*) is to praise it or express admiration. The nouns work the same way: a *complement* is something that completes the whole, whereas you pay someone a *compliment.* (*Complement* has a few other meanings—two angles that make up ninety degrees are complementary; a ship can have a full complement of sailors; the words after a verb are often called a complement—but these are the important ones for most everyday use.)

COMPOUND WORDS.

Linguists use the term *agglutination* for the process of putting together pieces of a long word, such as with AFFIXES and infixes. Some languages are far more agglutinative than English—in Turkish, I'm told, you can have a single word that means "Those of our number with whom we cannot exchange the season's greetings." But we do have a fair number of affixes like *un-, pre-, post-, -ness, -ment,* and so on, all of which allow us to form new words. We also can create new words by sticking complete old words together: think of *doorknob, backpack, racketball, self-service, editor-in-chief, month-long.*

A few things are worth observing carefully. First, although in theory you can create new compound words (see NEOLOGISM), you should usually resist the urge, unless you're convinced your audience will receive them well. Long compound words can be difficult to follow, and new ones won't be familiar to anyone. Second, it's not always clear when to use a HYPHEN between the various parts: notice that the examples in the previous paragraph include some with hyphens and some without. How to tell?—although there are some guidelines, it's easier simply to turn to a DICTIONARY than to try to remember all the possibilities. And note that sometimes hyphenation is a matter of HOUSE STYLE: you might see *goodwill*, *good-will*, and *good will* in different publications; *frontrunner* competes with *front-runner* and *startup* with *start-up*.

We're accustomed thinking of ADJECTIVES as single words: *good*, *hot*, *fast*. But a phrase can also function as an adjective: think of *middle-class morality*, *eighteenth-century art*, *thin-skinned writers*, *law-and-order candidate*, *up-to-the-minute news*, *behind-the-scene negotiations*, *one-size-fits-all solutions*. These compound adjectives usually get HYPHENS between the components that make them up. For more details, though, see PREDICATE.

See also WEB SITE.

COMPRISE.

Comprise traditionally means *comprehend* or *contain*, not *constitute*. In other words, a zoo comprises animals—it's not comprised of them (though it is *composed of* them). It's therefore wise to avoid the phrase *is comprised of* in formal writing.

Examples:

Disputed: The league is comprised of eight teams.

Preferred: The league comprises eight teams.
or
The league consists of eight teams.

CONCRETE LANGUAGE.

Writing is almost always more effective when you use specific, concrete words instead of vague, abstract ones. Instead of "apparent significant financial gains," use "a lot of money" or "large profits." Instead of "Job suffers a series of unfavorable experiences," use "Job's family is killed and his possessions are destroyed." Be PRECISE.

CONFUSED PAIRS.

Many entries in this guide are concerned with words that are easily confused. For ease of reference, I've collected most of them here. Scan the list and, if you're not confident you know the differences, read the entries. To make matters simple, I've usually alphabetized them in this guide under the first word in the pair.

affect and *effect*

alternate and *alternative*

among and *between*

anxious and *eager*

anymore and *any more*

as and *like*

assure, ensure, and *insure*

climactic and *climatic*

complement and *compliment*

continual and *continuous*

e.g. and *i.e.*

economic and *economical*

everyday and *every day*

farther and *further*

flammable and *inflammable*

flaunt and *flout*

historic and *historical*

> *imply* and *infer*
>
> *incredible* and *incredulous*
>
> *it's* and *its*
>
> *lay* and *lie*
>
> *lead* and *led*
>
> *lend* and *loan*
>
> *loath* and *loathe*
>
> *loose* and *lose*
>
> *orient* and *orientate*
>
> *principal* and *principle*
>
> *than* and *then*
>
> *therefore* and *therefor*
>
> *toward* and *towards*
>
> *who* and *whom*
>
> *whose* and *who's*

You'll find the details under each entry.

Conjunctions.

Conjunctions—the word comes from *conjoin*, "put together"—are little words that connect various elements in a sentence. They come in two flavors. You're probably already familiar with the *coordinating conjunctions*: the most common are *and*, *but*, *or*, and *nor*. Coordinating conjunctions connect two things of the same kind: two nouns ("cats *and* dogs"), two verbs ("kicks *or* screams"), two adjectives ("short *and* sweet"), two adverbs ("quickly *but* carefully"), or even two independent clauses ("Dylan writes better songs, *but* Britney sells more records").

Another kind of conjunction, the *subordinating conjunction*, is a little more troublesome. It joins entire clauses, but one is *principal*, the other *subordinate* ("subordinate" means something like "secondary" or "under the control of"). A subordinating conjunction joins an independent clause to a dependent one, and it's the conjunction that makes the dependent clause dependent. An example will make it clearer. Take two independent clauses: "I went to the doctor" and "I feel rotten." We can glue them together with a coordinating conjunction: "I went to the doctor *and* I feel rotten." This is clear enough, though it doesn't really suggest the connection between the two; *and* just serves the same function as a period between two sentences. A subordinating conjunction, though, shows their relation: "I went to the doctor *because* I feel rotten" (the subordinating conjunction *because* shows a causal connection); "*Because* I went to the doctor, I feel rotten" (another causal connection, but it's the other way around now); "*Although* I went to the doctor, I feel rotten"; "I went to the doctor, *even though* I feel rotten"; and so on. A complete list of subordinating conjunctions is very long, but includes *after*, *although*, *as if*, *because*, *before* (but *before* can also be an adverb or a PREPOSITION), *if*, *notwithstanding*, *since*, *so* (in the sense of "with the result that"), *that* (as in "I'm surprised *that* you're here"), *until*, *whenever*, *whereas*, and *why* (as in "I wonder *why* he did that").

In formal writing, avoid using *like* as a conjunction—you mean *as* or *as if*. *Like* is fine as a preposition ("My love is *like* a red, red rose," "He works *like* a madman"), but don't use it before a clause ("She's trying *like* [should be *as if*] there's no tomorrow"). See AS *VERSUS* LIKE.

CONNOTATION *VERSUS* DENOTATION.

A *denotation* is a word's *literal* meaning; a *connotation* is the full range of suggestions and associations that go with it. Dictionaries usually give a word's denotations, but are less useful in revealing connotations; a good writer, though, has to be conscious of the hidden meanings carried by every word. Think, for instance, about the phrases *make love, have intercourse, make whoopie, copulate, mate,* and *screw*—they all refer to the same act, but they're not at all interchangeable. When you need to refer to the act, you have to figure out which set of associations will have the desired effect on your audience. It's the same with other words: is someone a *rebel*, a *freedom-fighter*, a *criminal*, a *traitor*?—*overweight, heavy, chubby, hefty,* or *obese*?—*principled* or *stubborn*?—*unaware* or *oblivious*? Make your choices carefully. See AUDIENCE, DICTION, DICTIONARIES, and THESAURUS.

CONSIDERED AS, CONSIDERED TO BE.

Often useless. "The section is considered as essential" or "The section is considered to be essential" just add extra syllables to "The section is considered essential." Even better, ask yourself whether the word *considered* does anything in the sentence— does it matter who is considering? "The section is essential" is best of all.

CONTINUAL *VERSUS* CONTINUOUS.

Continual means "happening over and over again"; *continuous* means "happening constantly without stopping." If you're *continually* on the Internet, it means you keep going on; if you're *continuously* on the Internet, it means you haven't gone off at all.

CONTRACTIONS.

Contractions (such as *it's, they're, aren't, don't, she'd*) are usually less FORMAL than the expanded forms (*it is, they are, are not, do not, she would*). Whether you use them, then, depends on context—which is to say, on AUDIENCE. My own inclination is to be less rather than more formal in most college-level writing, but you'll have to judge that for yourself.

Note, though, that *cannot* is always one word.

CORPUS.

Although *corpus* is a Latin noun and it still takes a Latin PLURAL, but it doesn't belong to the class of nouns that takes a plural in *-i*. The proper plural is *corpora*, not *corpi*. See also APPARATUS, GENIUS, GENUS, OPUS, and VIRUS.

Could[n't] Care Less.

See clichés.

Could Of, Should Of, Would Of.

No: the expressions are *could have, should have, would have.*
We tend to pronounce unstressed syllables with a schwa
sound, and the *h* at the beginning of the word *have* often
disappears, meaning it's hard to tell *could have* from *could of*
in spoken English. (We often express this spoken form with a
contraction like *could've.*) In writing, though, it's important
to use the proper form.

Count *versus* Mass Nouns.

English nouns can be divided into two categories: *count nouns*
take a plural; *mass nouns* don't.

Mass nouns are words like *water, air, knowledge, music, traffic,
software,* and so on: you can't count them; you just consider
them as a mass of stuff. (What are "two airs"? How can you
count "musics"?) Count nouns, on the other hand, are words
like *song, book, hockey puck, mother-in-law,* and so on: it makes
sense to speak of one or several.

Some nouns can go either way. *Hair,* for instance, is a mass
noun in "He has very little hair left," but it's a count noun in
"He has only four hairs left on his head"—the difference is
whether we're concerned with individual strands. Ditto *fire*: it
can be stuff ("Fire kills thousands of people every year") or it
can be things ("The department extinguished six major fires
last month alone")—the difference is whether we're concerned
with individual outbreaks of fire. "I like opera" means "I
like the whole genre," so *opera* there is a mass noun; "I like
Puccini's operas" means "I like specific examples of the genre,"
so it's a count noun. Even something like *water*—almost
always a mass noun—can be considered a count noun if you're
comparing different brands of bottled water, or if a waitress is
asked to take "five waters" to table 27. (In these cases, a count
noun is usually hiding: "*kinds* of water," "*glasses* of water," and
so on.)

Sometimes it's not obvious whether something is a count or a mass noun. *Furniture*, for instance, seems to refer to discrete things, but it's still a mass noun; you can have "many *pieces* of furniture," but it makes no sense to talk about "many furnitures." *Money* is even more difficult to understand: yes, you can count money, but we still refer to an "*amount* of money," not a "*number* of moneys," so *money* is a mass noun. (It doesn't matter whether the plural is regular or irregular: it's *one deer, two deer*, but *deer* is still a count name, since you can have more than one of them; it doesn't matter that there's no *s*.)

Most of this is easy for native speakers of English, but you have to avoid a few traps. "A lot" works with both mass nouns and count nouns: "a lot of people" (count noun), "a lot of pain" (mass noun). Ditto "more": you can talk about "more trees" (count noun) or "more energy" (mass noun). But other ways of expressing extent are different with the two kinds of nouns. For instance, you describe a *number of things* (count nouns) but an *amount of stuff* (mass nouns): it's "the number of people" but "the amount of pain." And while you can talk about "more trees" (count noun) or "more energy" (mass noun), the opposite is "*fewer* trees" (count nouns take *fewer*) but "*less* energy" (mass nouns take *less*). You have the same split with *many* and *much*: it's "many trees" (count noun) but "much energy" (mass noun).

See AMOUNT and FEWER *VERSUS* LESS.

CURRENTLY.

What's wrong with *now*? Or even leaving it out altogether and letting a present-tense verb do the trick? *It is currently not available* is the same as *It is not available* or *It is not yet available*.

See also PRESENTLY.

DAILY BASIS.

See ON A ——— BASIS.

DANGLING PARTICIPLE.

A present participle is a verb ending in *-ing*, and is called *dangling* when the subject of the *-ing* verb and the subject of the sentence do not AGREE. An example is "Rushing to finish the paper, Bob's printer broke." Here the subject is *Bob's printer*, but the printer isn't doing the *rushing*. Better would be "While Bob was rushing to finish the paper, his printer broke." (Pay close attention to sentences beginning with *When ———ing*.)

One way to tell whether the participle is dangling is to put the phrase with the participle right after the subject of the sentence: "Bob's printer, rushing to finish the paper, broke" doesn't sound right.

Not all words ending in *-ing* are participles: in the sentence "Answering the questions in chapter four is your next assignment," the word *answering* functions as a noun, not a verb. (These nouns in *-ing* are called *gerunds*.)

Examples:

Disputed: Walking home the other day, a car nearly hit me.

Preferred: While I was walking home the other day, a car nearly hit me.

DASH.

A dash (publishers call it an "em-dash" because it's the width of the letter *m*) is used to mark a parenthesis—like this—or an interruption. Don't confuse it with a HYPHEN, although you can use two hyphens -- like this -- for dashes in your papers. (Virtually all word processors can produce a special symbol for the dash, which you can use if you like; note, though, that it's not always possible in every program, and they don't always come through in E-mail.) Whether dashes should have — spaces — around — them or not—like—this is a question of HOUSE STYLE.

There's nothing wrong with a few dashes here and there, but too many of them will make your writing less FORMAL. If you're aiming for a more elevated tone, use them sparingly whenever other punctuation marks are available.

I mentioned em-dashes; there are also en-dashes (as wide as the letter *n*), which are much more obscure. Professional typesetters often use en-dashes instead of hyphens to separate ranges (A–Z, pages 12–18) and for compounds made up of multiple words (Civil War–era weapons). Some, especially in Britain, used spaced en-dashes – like this – instead of the more familiar em-dashes. Unless you're doing serious typesetting, though, you needn't worry about them.

DATA.

Though it's nearly a lost cause, purists prefer to keep this a PLURAL noun: "The data *are*," not "the data *is*." The (now nearly obsolete) singular is *datum*. See also MEDIA and AGREEMENT.

DATES.

There's no single way to spell out dates; it's a matter of HOUSE STYLE. In American usage, "September 14, 2004" (usually with a comma) is most common when you're spelling things out, and "9/14/04" (or "09/14/04") when you're abbreviating. In much of the rest of the world, "14 September 2004" (usually without a comma) and "14/9/04" (or "14/09/04") are more common. Other possibilities abound, including some styles that put the year first. Whatever you do, be consistent; and if your audience might be international, avoid using just the digits: "04/03/02" could be 3 April 2002, 4 March 2002, 2 March 2004, and so on.

Decimate.

The word comes from a singularly gruesome practice in ancient Rome: when a legion engaged in mutiny, the rulers would execute every tenth man as a warning to the rest. Literally, then, it means to kill one out of ten, as the root *deci-* suggests (think *decimal*). It's now commonly used for anything that wipes out a large proportion of a population. Some readers dislike the more extended sense, preferring to limit it to things where about one-tenth gets destroyed, so use it with care.

Definite Articles.

See ARTICLES.

Demagogue.

I was surprised to discover that *demagogue* has been a verb since 1656—I assumed it was a recent mutation. Still, it's an ugly, JARGONY verb, one that no one but dimwitted politicians will miss. I notice that fully 94 percent of the *American Heritage Dictionary*'s usage panel reject it—good for them.

Dependent *versus* Independent Clauses.

A *clause* is a group of words with a subject and a verb, a part of a sentence. Some groups of words can get by on their own without any help: these are called *independent*. Others can't stand alone; either they don't have their own subject and verb, or they're subordinated to another part of the sentence: these are *dependent*. (A hint: dependent clauses often begin with words like *if, whether, since*, and so on; see CONJUNCTIONS.) Knowing the difference can help you figure out when to use COMMAS.

For example: in the sentence "Since we've fallen a week behind, we'll skip the second paper," the first part—"Since we've fallen a week behind"—is dependent, because it can't be a sentence on its own. The second part—"We'll skip the second paper"—does just fine on its own; it's an independent clause. The independent clause can be a sentence without any help from the *Since* clause.

A proper declarative sentence needs at least one independent clause. If it doesn't include a subject and a verb, or if it's introduced with a subordinating conjunction, it's a SENTENCE FRAGMENT.

DESCRIPTIVE GRAMMAR.

See PRESCRIPTIVE *VERSUS* DESCRIPTIVE GRAMMARS.

DIALOGUE.

Dialogue has been a verb for a long time; Shakespeare used it in 1607. But today its use as a verb sounds jargony—"He encouraged his partners to dialogue with one another"—and I encourage you to avoid it. The *American Heritage Dictionary* put the question to its usage panel; fully ninety-eight percent found it objectionable.

DICTION.

Diction means simply "word choice." English teachers probably mention it most often when there's a problem with the *level* of diction. Our language sports many near SYNONYMS, groups of which may share more or less the same denotation, but which differ in connotation. And sometimes these connotations can be arranged hierarchically, from high to low. Think of *warrior* (high diction), *soldier* (middle), and *dogface* or *grunt* (low); or *apparel* (high), *clothes* (middle), and *duds* (low). Higher diction often involves Latinate words, and lower diction Germanic, but not always.

It's not just a matter of high, middle, and low diction, though; there are many possible registers—scientific, flowery, bureaucratic, vulgar. The important thing is to be consistent: if you jump at random between levels of diction, you're likely to confuse your AUDIENCE. And that's a bad thing.

See CONNOTATION *VERSUS* DENOTATION, SYNONYMS, and THESAURUS.

DICTIONARIES.

No writer can survive without a good dictionary—you should probably own a few, and if you write for a living you should have a whole shelf full of them. Keep at least one close to where you write; keep another anywhere you do a lot of reading. Keep a pocket dictionary in your backpack or briefcase. Get into the habit of looking things up. It'll make you a better writer and a better reader.

Bookshops are packed with more dictionaries than I can count. Some are wonderful, some are a waste of paper. I'm fond of the *American Heritage Dictionary*, 4th ed.; it not only provides clear definitions, but refers controversial usage questions to a panel of experts who vote on whether the usage is acceptable. (It's also available for free on-line.) For more serious historical work, there's nothing like the *Oxford English Dictionary* (or *OED*, as it's universally known)—this twenty-volume behemoth not only provides remarkably comprehensive definitions, but it shows how words have been used throughout their history. Anyone who writes for a living—or even a hobby—should get to know the *OED*.

What about on-line dictionaries? As with print dictionaries, some are good, some are bad. A few of the major print dictionaries are available unabridged on the Web, some for free, some for an annual subscription charge. Others exist only on-line. Spend some time checking them out, and get a feel for their characteristic strengths and weaknesses. Don't assume a simple Google search will take the place of a reliable dictionary.

But while dictionaries are indispensable, you have to know how to use them. Be careful not to accord to them more authority than they claim for themselves: they're works of reference put together by people, not stone tablets engraved by God. The old argument that something is "not a word" because it doesn't appear in "the" dictionary (as if there were only one dictionary) is downright silly. Any pronounceable combination of letters to which someone assigns a meaning can be called a word; the question is whether it's a *good* word—by which, of course, I mean an *appropriate* word. Many dictionaries list words like *ain't* or *irregardless*; that doesn't mean you can use them with impunity in formal writing. Pay close attention to the usage notes—"Nonstandard," "Slang," "Vulgar"—and be sure you choose the right word.

Dictionaries are also more concerned with *denotations* than *connotations*, and you're a fool if you think a dictionary entry amounts to a Get-Out-of-Jail-Free card in any writing problem. Some dictionary may define *gook* as an Asian or *queen* as a gay man, but you can point to the dictionary all you like ("It's sense 3b!") without convincing anyone it's appropriate or inoffensive. Be sensitive to the associations your words carry to your audience.

One other note. Avoid referring to "Webster's," which has no specific meaning—any dictionary can use that name. Merriam-Webster, on the other hand, is a specific company that produces well-regarded dictionaries. Besides, dictionary definitions at the beginnings of papers rarely add anything to the discussion. A favorite line from *The Simpsons*, where Homer wins the First Annual Montgomery Burns Award for Outstanding Achievement in the Field of Excellence: "Webster's Dictionary defines 'excellence' as 'The quality or condition of being excellent.'" A well-chosen nugget of information from a dictionary is wonderful, especially when you're engaging in close reading, but you just waste your introduction if you use it to state the obvious.

See also THESAURUS.

DIFFERENT.

The word *different* is often redundant, as in *several different options* or *many different participants*. Since you can't have several of the same option or many of the same participant, *several options* and *many participants* will do nicely.

Note that the phrase "different than" gets under many people's skin. In most cases, "different *from*" is more widely acceptable. So "Grunge is different *from* heavy metal" (but "Things are different *than* they were"). Brits sometimes use "different *to*," but that sounds odd to American ears.

Examples:

Disputed: The leading concerns in women's health are different than those in men's health.

Preferred: The leading concerns in women's health are different from those in men's health.

DIRECT AND INDIRECT OBJECTS.

A direct object is the thing (or person) acted on by a TRANSITIVE verb. The indirect object is used most often for the recipient in verbs of giving. Examples are clearer than definitions.

"I took the paper"—*the paper* is the direct object, because the verb *took* acts on *the paper*; *the paper* is the thing that was taken. "I called her this morning"—*her* is the direct object, because the verb *called* acts on *her*; *her* is the person who was *called*.

"I gave him my suggestions" is a bit more complicated. Here *him* is an *indirect object*, because *him* isn't the thing that was *given*; I gave *suggestions*, and I gave them *to him*. *Suggestions* is the direct object, *him* the indirect object.

DISINTERESTED *VERSUS* UNINTERESTED.

The words are often used interchangeably, but traditionalists prefer to keep them separate. Both mean "without interest," but "interest" has several meanings.

Disinterested means "without a stake in"—without a bias, impartial. *Uninterested* means "indifferent" or "without a care about"—you just don't give a damn.

You can be *disinterested* in something but not *uninterested*, and vice versa. For instance, because I'm not a betting man, I don't stand to gain or lose anything in the outcome of most sporting events; I might still enjoy watching a game: I'm *disinterested* but not *uninterested*. Conversely, I might not care about the intricacies of tax policies, but I certainly have a stake in the outcome: I'm *uninterested* but not *disinterested*.

DISRESPECT.

The word *disrespect* as a verb—to *disrespect someone*—became newly fashionable in colloquial English, especially in hip-hop culture, in the 1990s, especially in the abridged form *to diss* or *dis*. Many traditionalists objected to this usage, insisting that you could *show disrespect to* but you couldn't *disrespect* someone. But *disrespect* has been a verb since 1614, and has been used by such authors as Tom Paine in 1791, Leigh Hunt in 1852, and George Meredith in 1876.

So it's not really a hot-off-the-presses NEOLOGISM, but it's worth bearing in mind that there are still readers who find it improper. The distaste says less about the word itself than about the traditionalists' distaste for the hip-hop culture in which the word became fashionable. So bear in mind that *to disrespect* has a long and respectable history, but its association with "street" culture makes some people suspicious of it. Make your decisions about using it accordingly.

The shorter form, *diss* or *dis*, really *is* a neologism; it's probably inappropriate in FORMAL contexts, though perfectly acceptable if you're being casual.

DIVE, DIVED, DOVE.

The traditional past-tense form of *dive* is *dived*. Although *dove* is common in speech, it's safer to stick with *dived* in writing. See also SNEAK, SNEAKED, SNUCK.

DONE *VERSUS* FINISHED.

In formal writing, if your AUDIENCE might include sticklers, it's a good idea to make the traditional distinction: "it's done," but "I've finished." In less formal situations, though, there's no need to get uptight about it.

DOUBLE GENITIVES.

English often uses a construction that strikes people as irrational, the "double genitive," which seems, illogically, to have two possessives in a row. The classic example is "a friend of mine"—logic says it should be "a friend of *me*," not "of *mine*." But logic isn't always the best guide to the English language, and the usage is widespread. Kenneth Wilson's *Columbia Guide to Standard American English* wags its finger, saying the construction is "now limited to our Informal and Semiformal writing and to the lowest levels of our speech." "It's either *friends of my sister*," writes Wilson, "or *my sister's friends*; even in conversation, *friends of my sister's* may grate harshly on some purists' ears." I'm not convinced; my sense is that the construction is so firmly established as an IDIOM that there's no point in complaining about it.

DOUBLE NEGATIVES.

In many languages, double negatives are perfectly acceptable: Spanish *no sé nada*, literally "I don't know nothing," means "I know nothing" or "I don't know anything." And in England, shortly before 1400, Chaucer wrote of his Knight, "Ther nas no man no wher so vertuous," which is literally "There wasn't no man nowhere so virtuous"—which we'd have to render today as "There was no man anywhere so virtuous."

So even in English, double negatives were once common. In Standard Modern English, though, they're problematic. Since the seventeenth century or so, people have been applying strict logic to these double negatives, suggesting that they "cancel each other out." Take the idiomatic Spanish phrase, "I don't know nothing": logic says that if you *don't* know *nothing*, then you *must* know *something*. As a result, it's usually best to avoid double negatives in formal writing.

As to whether two negatives "make a positive," that's a little more troublesome: you need to be sure you have an audience that will recognize your meaning. Ambiguity is always a danger in writing: there are two ways to pronounce "I couldn't do nothing," one of which is an informal way of saying "I couldn't do anything," the other "I couldn't sit by and do nothing, but had to get involved." Without the clues provided by spoken emphasis, though, your readers might not know which of these meanings you want to convey. Be careful.

DUE TO THE FACT THAT.

Some object to the phrase *due to* when it's used as a PREPOSITION: "He stayed home due to the flu." I don't much like it myself—I find it inelegant, and avoid it in my own speech and writing—but it's so widespread that it may be futile to campaign against it anymore. (Note, though, that it's *due to*, not *do to*.)

But the big, ugly phrase *due to the fact that* really has to go— not because of some abstract grammatical law, but because it's a stuffy, five-syllable way of saying "because." Remember, ECONOMY is a virtue.

DYSPHEMISM.

See EUPHEMISM.

Each.

A singular noun phrase, which requires a singular verb. Don't write "Each of the chapters *have* a title"; use "Each of the chapters *has* a title" or (better) "Each chapter *has* a title." See also EVERY.

Examples:

Wrong: Each of the employees get ten days off.

Right: Each of the employees gets ten days off.
  or
  Each employee gets ten days off.
  or
  Every employee gets ten days off.

Economic *versus* Economical.

They're not interchangeable. The adjective *economic* refers to the economy; *economical* refers to something that saves you money or is a good buy. See -IC AND -ICAL.

Economics.

For whether to treat it as singular or plural, see POLITICS.

Economy.

A distinguishing mark of clear and forceful writing is *economy* of style—using no more words than necessary. Bureaucratic and academic writing likes to pad every sentence with *It should continuously be remembered that*s and *Moreover, it has been previously indicated*s. Don't. It makes for flaccid prose. After you write a sentence, look it over and ask whether the sense would be damaged by judicious trimming. If not, start cutting, because the shorter version is usually better. Become friendly with the "Delete Word" option on your word processor. See WASTED WORDS.

ELLIPSES.

The ellipsis (the plural is *ellipses*) is the mark that indicates the omission of quoted material, as in "Brevity is…wit" (stolen shamelessly from *The Simpsons*). Note two things: first, most typing manuals and house styles prefer the periods to be spaced. (In electronic communication it's sometimes convenient, even necessary, to run them together, since line-wrap can be unpredictable.) Second, and more important, is the *number* of periods. The ellipsis itself is *three* periods (always); it can appear next to other punctuation, including an end-of-sentence period (resulting in *four* periods). Use four only when the words on either side of the ellipsis make full sentences. You should *never* use fewer than three or more than four periods, with only a single exception: when entire lines of poetry are omitted in a block quotation, it's a common practice to replace them with a full line of spaced periods.

One other thing. Although it's a matter of HOUSE STYLE, note that it's usually unnecessary to have ellipses at the *beginning* or *end* of a quotation; they're essential only when something's omitted in the *middle*. There's no need for "…this…" when "this" will do: readers will understand you're not quoting everything the source ever said, and that there will be material before and after the quotation you give. The only time it's advisable is when the bit you're quoting isn't grammatical when it's standing on its own: "When I was a boy…"—that sort of thing.

EFFECT *VERSUS* AFFECT.

See AFFECT *VERSUS* EFFECT.

E.G. *VERSUS* I.E.

The abbreviation *e.g.* is for the LATIN *exempli gratia*, "for example." *I.e.*, Latin *id est*, means "that is." They're not interchangeable. Most American style guides advise that both abbreviations should get periods and should be followed by a comma. And you don't need to put *etc.* after a list beginning with *e.g.*; since it promises just a few examples, it's understood the list isn't complete.

Examples:

Wrong: There are three branches of government, e.g., the executive, the legislative, and the judiciary.

The primate order includes dozens of species, i.e., lemurs, howler monkeys, chimpanzees, and gorillas.

Right: There are three branches of government, i.e., the executive, the legislative, and the judiciary.

The primate order includes dozens of species, e.g., lemurs, howler monkeys, chimpanzees, and gorillas.

E-MAIL, EMAIL, E-MAIL, EMAIL.

There's not much agreement yet on whether the *E* in *E-mail* should be capital or small, and whether it should get a hyphen. This means there are at least four forms circulating: *E-mail, Email, e-mail,* and *email.* (I've seen *eMail,* but not often.) It's a matter of HOUSE STYLE, and there probably won't be a clear standard for quite some time. I'm fond of the capital *E* and the hyphen (on the model of other words formed with initials, like *A-bomb* and *G-man*), but when have I ever gotten my way? See also ON-LINE *VERSUS* ONLINE and WEB-SITE.

Another question is whether *E-mails* is kosher—whether, in other words, we should treat it as a COUNT NOUN OR A MASS NOUN. The word *mail* is a mass noun: we don't speak of regular *mails,* but *pieces of mail.* I confess I still find *E-mails* (with or without capitals and hyphens) distracting, and I avoid it in my own writing. But it seems the public has spoken, and virtually every style guide smiles on *E-mails* for multiple pieces of E-mail.

EMOTICONS.

The little smiley doohickeys—things like :-) and its derivatives—are common in informal correspondence, especially in electronic communication like E-mail and text messages. They'd be out of place in FORMAL WRITING, though. A good writer lets words do all the hard work.

Emphasis.

There are several ways to draw attention to passages in your writing that deserve special emphasis. I'll start, though, with a few means you should avoid.

First, never resort to ALL CAPITALS in formal writing. Bigger Type is also out; likewise **boldface**. They all come across as amateurish—note how rarely you see them in published prose. Professionals know that they're counterproductive. (Here I'm talking just about the body of text: boldface, caps, and larger type are permissible in section headings and things like that.) And exclamation points have to be used very sparingly.

So what's left?—Italics (or underscore; the two are interchangeable) can draw attention to a word or a short phrase, though even this should be used with care. *Use* it when you *want* to highlight a *short* passage, but *don't* resort to it *over* and *over* again, or it *loses* its *effect*.

The best way to draw attention to particular passages, though, is to construct your sentences to put the important words in the most prominent places. A tip: the strongest positions in a sentence are the beginning and the end. Don't waste this prime real estate on transitional words like *however, additionally, moreover, therefore*, and so on. Instead of "*However*, the paper was finished on time" or "The paper was finished on time, *however*," save the beginning and end of your sentences for more important stuff like nouns and verbs. Try "The paper, *however*, was finished on time."

England.

See Britain.

ENORMITY.

Enormity is etymologically related to *enormous*, but it has a more specific meaning: it's used for things that are tremendously *wicked* or *evil*, things that pass all moral bounds. You can use it to describe genocides and such, but it's not the same as *enormousness* or *immensity*. Saying things like "the enormity of the senator's victory" when you mean simply the great size is likely to confuse people. See also FULSOME and OFFICIOUS.

EPIC.

Too often used as a CLICHÉ for anything with a big sweep—it seems that any movie with a cast of more than ten is described as "epic." Better is to restrict the word to things that are truly related to the epic tradition—y'know, Homer, Virgil, Milton, all that stuff.

E-PRIME.

E-Prime (or E')—the "E" stands for "English," and the "prime" comes from mathematics, where it indicates one variable's close relation to another (for derivatives, transformations, and set complements, for example)—designates a variety of English that uses no verbs of being. Some writers try to avoid *all* verbs of being, favoring the more forceful ACTION VERBS in their place. So a book written in E-Prime includes no occurrences of *to be* in any of its forms.

Overuse of verbs of being makes writing lifeless, and no one should object to more action verbs. In fact, beginning writers may profit from the exercise of removing all the verbs of being from their writing, since it forces them to find more forceful means of expression. Inflexibly applying *any* rule, though, savors of pedantry, and your fear of BUGBEARS should never lead you into gracelessness. I've written this entry in E-Prime, and its occasional clumsiness reveals the dangers of riding any hobbyhorse too seriously. See ACTION VERBS, EXISTS, and PASSIVE VOICE.

EQUALLY AS.

Don't. Something can be *equally important*, or it can be *as important*, but it can't be *equally as important*.

Examples:

Wrong: The two are equally as difficult.

The poorly made one is equally as expensive as the good one.

Right: The two are equally difficult.

The poorly made one is as expensive as the good one.

or

The poorly made one is just as expensive as the good one.

ESSENTIALLY.

See BASICALLY and WASTED WORDS.

ET AL.

See ETC.

ETC.

LATIN *et*, "and," *cetera*, "other [things]." If you want to refer to other people, rather than things, the usual abbreviation is *et al.*, for "et alia." Since *al.* is an abbreviation, you need the period. Remember that *et cetera* is abbreviated *etc.*, not *ect.*

You might see *&c.* in some older books. The AMPERSAND (&) originally began as a scribal shorthand for Latin *et*, so *&c.* is just an old-fashioned form of *etc.*

ETHICS.

For whether to treat it as singular or plural, see POLITICS.

ETHNICITY.

See AFRICAN AMERICAN, AMERICA, NATIONALITY, and POLITICALLY LOADED LANGUAGE.

EUPHEMISM.

From Greek: *eu*, "good" or "well"; *pheme*, "saying." A euphemism is a delicate way of saying something that might be offensive: instead of *fat*, for instance, you might say *plump*; instead of *buttocks*, you might say *tush*. (The opposite is *dysphemism*, a much less common word, for particularly brash words, like *brat* for *child*, *screw-up* for *mistake*, *fogey* for *elderly*, or *crackpot* for *insane*. Two linguists, Keith Allan and Kate Burridge, have proposed the term *orthophemism* for neutral words with neither positive nor negative CONNOTATIONS, but that one hasn't yet caught on.)

Use euphemisms with care. It would be crass to use dysphemisms like *croak* or *kick the bucket* at a funeral; we protect the feelings of the mourners with euphemisms like *departed* or *passed on*. Fair enough—no one wants to make the bereaved feel worse than they do already. But the euphemism habit often goes too far. Some people go through all sorts of verbal contortions to avoid using a perfectly decent word like *toilet*: *bathroom* (even when there's no bath), *powder room*, *washroom*, *restroom*, *little girls' room*, and so on. (A favorite line from Edward Albee's play, *Who's Afraid of Virginia Woolf*: "Martha, won't you show her where we keep the… euphemism?") Don't be squeamish. And politicians and others often resort to euphemisms to hide things that would otherwise provoke horror. Military terms like *inflicting collateral damage* (for accidentally killing civilians) and corporate terms like *let go* (for fired) often allow people to get away with shameful behavior. Strive to be direct.

See also POLITICALLY LOADED LANGUAGE.

EVERY.

Every requires a singular verb and singular pronouns. Don't write "Every one of the papers *have* been graded"; use "Every one of the papers *has* been graded" or (better) "Every paper has been graded." Ditto *everyone*: "Everyone must sign *his or her* name," not "*their* name." See also EACH and SEXIST LANGUAGE.

Examples:

Disputed: Every student needs their own computer.

Preferred: Every student needs his or her own computer

or

All students need their own computers.

Every Day *versus* Everyday.

Keep 'em straight: *everyday* (one word) is an adjective, and means "normal, quotidian, not out of the ordinary." Other senses should be two words. So: if an event happens every day, you might consider it an everyday event.

Examples:

Wrong: The sun comes up everyday.

It's an every day occurrence.

Right: The sun comes up every day.

It's an everyday occurrence.

Exclamation Points.

Go easy on them, okay? They can add EMPHASIS to a sentence, but using too many looks amateurish. They give the impression of breathlessness, of wide-eyed wonder—and to readers, the subject may not seem to warrant that degree of wonderment. If you always seem to be shouting, your audience will stop listening. Understatement is usually more effective. If, after these cautions, you decide an exclamation point is still the way to go, stop at one. You almost *never* need more than a single exclamation point to make your point.

Exists.

Unless you're a professional phenomenologist, you can live very comfortably without the word *exists* in your vocabulary. Instead of saying "A problem *exists* with the system," say "*There is* a problem with the system" (or, maybe even better, "The system doesn't work"—see ACTION VERBS).

Extracts.

See BLOCK QUOTATIONS.

FACET.

The METAPHOR is often abused. Don't use a *facet*, the hard polished side of a gem, to stand in for the more general "aspect" unless it's really appropriate.

THE FACT THAT.

Usually unnecessary. You can often simply drop *the fact* and go with *that* alone: instead of "I'm surprised by *the fact that* the report is incomplete," write "I'm surprised *that* the report is incomplete" (or even "I'm surprised the report is incomplete"). And don't be afraid to rewrite the sentence altogether.

FACTOR.

A word beloved by business types, but often with precious little meaning. There's probably a more PRECISE word. Look for it.

FARTHER *VERSUS* FURTHER.

Though few people bother with the difference these days, there is a traditional distinction: *farther* applies to physical distance, *further* to metaphorical distance. You travel *farther*, but pursue a topic *further*. Don't get upset if you can't keep it straight; no one will notice.

FEEL.

The use of *feel* for words like *think*, *believe*, and *argue* is becoming unsettlingly common. It's a cliché, and a touchy-feely one at that, reducing all cognition to sensation and emotion. When I see sentences beginning "Wittgenstein feels that…" or "Socrates feels he is…" I start to feel queasy. Avoid it.

FEWER *VERSUS* LESS.

They're easily confused, because they're both the opposite of *more*, but *more* has two meanings, one for a greater amount of stuff, the other for a greater number of things. *Less* means "not as much"; *fewer* means "not as many." Once you understand the principle, you can usually trust your ear: if you'd use "much," use "less"; if you'd use "many," use "fewer." You earn *less* money by selling *fewer* products; you use *less* oil but eat *fewer* fries. If you can count them, use *fewer*.

For more information, see COUNT *VERSUS* MASS NOUNS.

Examples:

Disputed: This page has less words on it than the other one.
Preferred: This page has fewer words on it than the other one.
or
This page has less text on it than the other one.

FIANCÉ, FIANCÉE.

Fiancé, a man engaged to be married; *fiancée*, a woman engaged to be married. It usually retains the ACCENT even though it's by now a familiar English word.

FINALIZE.

An ugly, JARGONY word. Consider something more elegant and precise: *finishes?—brings to a close?—wraps up?*

FIRST(LY), SECOND(LY), THIRD(LY).

The jury is still out on whether to use *first* or *firstly*, *second* or *secondly*, and so on. Traditional usage had *first, secondly, thirdly*, but this has the disadvantage of being internally inconsistent. My recommendation is plain old *first, second, third*, and so forth, without the *-ly* ending.

FIRST PERSON.

See PERSON.

FLAMMABLE *VERSUS* INFLAMMABLE.

Despite appearances, they mean the same thing. In many words, the *in-* prefix means "not": think of *inedible, indirect,* or *inconceivable.* (Latin spelling rules—more than you have reason to care about—mean that it's essentially the same "not" prefix in *illegal, impossible,* and *irregular.*)

But the *in-* prefix on *inflammable* is different: instead of meaning "not," it's an intensifier. How are you supposed to tell the difference? Well, unless you're conversant in Latin, you just have to *know,* that's all. The word *inflammable* long predates *flammable*—1605 versus 1813 (the word *flammability* appeared in the seventeenth century, but it then disappeared until the twentieth). But in the twentieth century, *flammable* has been increasingly used to mean "able to be set on fire," and *inflammable* has been losing ground.

The problem is that the "real" meaning of the word (that is, the traditional meaning supported by most dictionaries) is the exact opposite of what many people assume it means. Now, with words like *comprise* or *enormity,* no one's life depends on dictionary entries. But someone trying to put out a fire who sees a bucket of something labeled "INFLAMMABLE" has good reason to hope for perfect clarity.

The practical lesson to take away from this entry: if you're reasonably certain everyone in your audience knows the "real" meaning of the word, feel free to use *inflammable* "correctly" to mean "able to be set on fire." And if you're writing metaphorically, it probably can't hurt to use *inflammable.* But if there's any chance some poor person is going to misunderstand you and go up in flames as a result, be as explicit as you can. *Flammable* and *not flammable* (or *nonflammable*) are probably your best bet. And if you're the one trying to put out a fire, avoid the bucket labeled "INFLAMMABLE."

Flaunt *versus* Flout.

The two words are easily CONFUSED, but they aren't interchangeable, and you'll look bad if you mix them up. To *flaunt* is to show off or display: you can flaunt your money and you can flaunt your knowledge of trivia. To *flout,* on the other hand, is to show contempt for something: you can flout a rule or flout a convention.

THE FOLLOWING.

See ABOVE.

FONTS.

Don't play with fonts: leave desktop publishing to the desktop publishers. Most publishers and professors don't want fancy fonts; they'd be content if your writing had been typed on a manual typewriter, circa 1958. Don't count on having readers who judge your work based on the typeface. If you're writing for a class, some instructors will care about the typeface you use; in those cases, follow their guidelines. Others won't; in those cases pick something simple and unobtrusive. Spend your time writing.

Oh—and *please* don't insult your professors' intelligence by padding out a too-short paper with gigantic typefaces, narrow margins, and wide line-spacing to make it seem longer. Despite all appearances to the contrary, we're *really* not that dumb.

See also JUSTIFICATION.

FOOTNOTES.

See the section on citation at the end of this book.

FOREGO *VERSUS* FORGO.

Both are real words, but they're not interchangeable. To *forego* (with an *e*) means "to go before"; the most common context is the expression "a foregone conclusion" (one you reached in advance). To *forgo* (no *e*) means "to do without" or "to abstain from."

FOREIGN WORDS AND PHRASES.

Foreign words and phrases shouldn't become a *bête noire*, but, *ceteris paribus*, English sentences should be in English. Clarity is the *sine qua non* of good writing, and the overuse of such words just confuses your readers—*satis, superque*. Remember, *Allzuviel ist nicht gesund*. Besides, there's nothing worse than trying to impress and getting it wrong. When it comes to foreign phrases, *chi non fa, non falla*. (*Das versteht sich von selbst*.)

For advice on the treatment of foreign words, see ITALICS.

FORMAL WRITING.

Many—most?—of the rules in this guide are concerned with *written* rather than *spoken* English, and, what's more, with written language of a certain degree of *formality*. That's to say, I'm trying to describe the kind of prose that's appropriate for a college English paper, which also happens to be the kind used in most business writing. Many no-no's in a college English paper, though, are perfectly acceptable in other contexts; novelists, for instance, would miss out on many fascinating varieties of English if they limited themselves to this style alone. Don't get dogmatic on me. See especially AUDIENCE, PRESCRIPTIVE *VERSUS* DESCRIPTIVE GRAMMARS, and RULES.

FORTUITOUS.

Fortuitous means "happening by chance," not necessarily a lucky chance. Don't use it interchangeably with *fortunate* or *lucky*.

FRAGMENTS.

See SENTENCE FRAGMENTS.

FREQUENTLY.

There's nothing wrong with the word, but it's just a long and Latinate way of saying *often*. Don't be afraid to use the shorter, more direct word.

FULSOME

Fulsome is one of those words that sounds value-neutral or even positive, but is actually negative. Although it's etymologically related to *full*, it has negative CONNOTATIONS—it usually means "overdone" or "too much." So "fulsome praise" suggests not "copious praise" but "too much praise." The more neutral meaning is in widespread use, but you should avoid it in formal writing. See also ENORMITY and OFFICIOUS.

FUNCTIONALITY.

Functionality is too often a twisted way of saying *function*. See also METHODOLOGY.

Gay.

See POLITICALLY LOADED LANGUAGE.

Gender.

Gender comes from the Latin *genus*, which means "kind"—any old kind of kind, not necessarily masculine and feminine. It was a technical term in grammar to describe the kinds of nouns and adjectives: in most European languages, they could be *masculine*, *feminine*, or (in a few languages) *neuter*.

According to the traditional distinction, nouns and adjectives have a *gender*, while people and animals have a *sex*. Language textbooks are careful to insist they're not the same thing: *masculine* isn't the same as *male*, nor is *feminine* the same as *female*. German *Weib*, for instance, means "wife," by definition female; the noun, though, is neuter. And in many languages the distribution of nouns into masculine, feminine, and neuter seems pretty arbitrary. The very fact that other languages like Swahili have more than three genders should remind us it's unwise to map gender onto sex.

In the twentieth century, though, feminist theorists began to use the word *gender* in a newish way, to distinguish biology from society. In this scheme, your plumbing determines your biological *sex*; your social role determines your *gender*. Most biological males behave in socially masculine ways; most biological women behave in socially feminine ways—but the distinction allows us to discuss people who don't follow the norms, including transgendered people, those with XXY chromosomes, and biological hermaphrodites. If you care to observe this distinction, feel free—it's often useful.

It's probably unwise, though, to allow *gender* to edge out *sex* altogether. Once *gender* began to be used to describe people, it became first a SYNONYM, and then a EUPHEMISM, for *sex*. The word *sex* still provokes giggles, and I can understand why people who prepare questionnaires would be glad to see it disappear after finding the "Sex" blank on a form filled in with "Yes, please" for the jillionth time. Still, using *gender* to refer to biological sex should be avoided, except where it avoids confusion or ambiguity.

In either the traditional system, in which *gender* applies only to grammatical categories, or the more recent feminist theory, in which it describes a social role, the word shouldn't be used to describe biology, for which *sex* has long been the preferred word. In practical terms: an ultrasound can't tell you the *gender* of a fetus, though it may tell you the *sex*. Cats and dogs don't have a gender, but they do have a sex.

GENERALIZATIONS.

Since the beginning of time, man has wrestled with the great questions of the universe. Humans have always sought to understand their place in creation. There is no society on earth that has not attempted to reckon with the human condition.

Balderdash. Generalizations like that are sure to sink your writing, because they almost always fall into one of two classes: the *obvious* and the *wrong*.

For starters, *how do you know* what has happened since the beginning of time?—is your knowledge of early *Australopithecus robustus* family structure extensive enough to let you compare it to Etruscan social organization? Have you read Incan religious texts alongside Baha'i tracts? Unless you've taken courses in omniscience, I'm guessing the answer's no. In that case, you're saying things you simply don't know, and certainly don't know any better than your audience. So it's either obvious to everyone, or a plain old lie.

Couching vacuous ideas in portentous prose impresses nobody. Simplicity, clarity, and precision will always win over ringing generalizations: don't think everything you write has to settle the mysteries of the ages in expressions worthy of Shakespeare. As Calvin Trillin puts it, "When a man has nothing to say, the worst thing he can do is to say it memorably."

GENIUS.

Genius comes from Latin, and it does in fact take the PLURAL *genii* in that language—but not in ours. The only acceptable English plural of *genius* is *geniuses*. See also CORPUS, GENUS, OPUS, and VIRUS.

GENUS.

The term for the classification above the SPECIES in biology is the *genus*. The *-us* at the end might suggest that Latin PLURAL should be *geni*—but it's not. It's actually *genera*, and that's the preferred form in English, too. See also CORPUS, GENIUS, OPUS, SPECIES, and VIRUS.

GERMANIC DICTION.

See LATINATE *VERSUS* GERMANIC DICTION.

GERUND.

See DANGLING PARTICIPLES.

GRACE.

Grace always trumps pedantry. Good writing is lively, engaging, compelling; it flows, and has no truck with RULES that interfere with readerly enjoyment. It's possible to follow every rule in a hundred grammar books and still write lifeless prose. In fact, following the rules too slavishly can suck the life out of your writing. Don't let rule-mongering make your prose unreadable. See BUGBEARS, AUDIENCE, CLARITY, PRESCRIPTIVE *VERSUS* DESCRIPTIVE GRAMMARS, and RULES.

GRAMMAR.

Grammar, strictly defined, is a comparatively narrow field: most questions native speakers have about a language deal not with *grammar* but with *usage* or *style*. Grammar is the more scientific aspect of the study of a language: it's made up of *morphology* (the forms words take, also known as *accidence*) and *syntax* (their relation to one another). Grammar gives names to the various PARTS OF SPEECH and their relations (see, in this guide, ADJECTIVES AND ADVERBS, ANTECEDENT, APPOSITION, CONJUNCTIONS, PREPOSITIONS, IMPERATIVE, PERSON, TRANSITIVE AND INTRANSITIVE VERBS, DIRECT AND INDIRECT OBJECTS, and AGREEMENT), so it's useful in providing a vocabulary to discuss how language works. But if you're debating whether language should be concrete, or where to put *only* in a sentence, or when to use italics—strictly speaking, that's a question of *usage* or *style* rather than grammar. And some come down to nothing more than TASTE.

Many linguists complain that the terms taught in school are inadequate for discussing the way our language really works. It's a fair cop: most of our grammatical categories are imported from Latin grammar, and often don't jibe well with English. Still, in this guide I tend to use the traditional terms. That's because few of my readers were taught the more modern system in school, which means explanations that depended on them would confuse rather than enlighten. Besides, the traditional terms are good enough to make the points I want to make here.

I should point out that this guide isn't intended to be a formal or systematic grammar, just a handy *vade mecum* (look it up) on effective style. I define grammatical terms only insofar as they're useful in improving usage. If you want *real* grammar, talk to the linguists, who know what they're talking about in a way I never will. (See PRESCRIPTIVE *VERSUS* DESCRIPTIVE GRAMMARS for further details.)

One more thing—for the love of Pete, *please* don't spell it "grammer," unless you put "Kelsey" right in front of it.

GRAMMAR CHECKERS.

I have no problem with SPELLING CHECKERS; while they sometimes miss typos, they rarely give advice that's downright *wrong*. Computerized *grammar* checkers, on the other hand, are a mess. They not only miss most of the serious problems, they actually give *wretched* advice, often telling you to fix something that's not broken. And of course they have no sense of GRACE, which means they can only apply RULES pedantically with no sense of context. I've played with many of them, and have never seen one worth the CD-ROM it's printed on.

A fun experiment is to take some great work of literature and feed it to a grammar checker, and then to see what mincemeat it makes of it. Here are some mindless tips on the first sentence of Milton's *Paradise Lost*:

> Consider revising. Very long sentences can be difficult to understand.
>
> Avoid contractions like "flow'd" in formal writing (consider "flow had").
>
> Avoid the use of "Man" (try "he or she").
>
> "One greater Man restore" has subject-verb agreement problems.
>
> "In the Beginning" should be "at first."
>
> "Or if Sion" should be "also if Sion."

And so on. Milton's style is judged appropriate for a 98th-grade reading level. (Well, okay, that seems about right. But the rest is silly.)

Maybe someday I'll be pleasantly surprised, but for now, rely on your own knowledge when you revise and proofread. See also SPELLING CHECKERS and MICROSOFT WORD.

GREAT BRITAIN.

See BRITAIN.

GROW.

This word arouses a lot of passion, though I really don't understand why. Some people get downright furious when they come across *grow* used as a TRANSITIVE verb. It became common when Bill Clinton made "grow the economy" part of his stump speech in the 1992 presidential elections, and since then it's become widespread in the media and in business writing.

Some people grumpily insist this usage is *wrong*, a perversion of the language that must be stamped out. The *economy grows*, they say, and you can even *make the economy grow*, but you can't *grow the economy*. The verb *grow*, they insist, is an intransitive verb, so it can't take a DIRECT OBJECT.

The problem with this argument is that neither logic, nor grammar, nor usage bears it out. People have been *growing corn* and *growing beards*—both examples of *grow* as a transitive verb—since at least 1774: they mean "cause to grow" or "allow to grow." There's no logical reason why you can't also *grow the economy*, or *grow* anything else you want to make bigger. The only unusual thing is that it's being applied to something that gets bigger metaphorically, rather than literally.

This doesn't mean you have to like the transitive *grow*, and you certainly don't have to use it. Since many people get uptight about it, I'd advise you to avoid it in most writing, since it's not yet completely naturalized Standard English. I find it ugly, and avoid it myself. But that's really a matter of TASTE, not of GRAMMAR. There's no better reason to exclude it from the language.

HEAVILY.

There's nothing wrong with the word, but it's overused as an all-purpose intensifier. If you're constructing a metaphor in which weight is appropriate—"heavily overloaded," for instance—it's fine. If not, try to find a more appropriate adverb, and your sentence will probably be more vivid as a result.

HELPING VERBS.

See AUXILIARY VERBS.

HISTORIC *VERSUS* HISTORICAL.

Both are adjectives derived from the noun *history*, but they have different applications. A *historic* event is one of great importance in history: "King's historic speech, 'I Have a Dream.'" A *historical* event is simply one that happened in the past. See -IC AND -ICAL.

HOI POLLOI.

Greek: *hoi*, nominative masculine plural of the article *ho*, "the"; *polloi*, nominative masculine plural of *polus*, "many." The phrase means "the common people, the masses." Don't confuse it with the upper classes—it has nothing to do with "high" or "hoity-toity."

The big controversy about *hoi polloi* in English—the sort of thing that raises blood pressures to dangerous levels—is whether you should say "*the* hoi polloi": *hoi* already means *the*, so "the hoi polloi" means "the the many." Then again, people have been saying "the hoi polloi" for as long as they've been using the expression in English (since 1668, says the *OED*). Besides, we say "the La Brea Tar Pits," even though that means "the the tar tar pits." And the *al* at the beginning of many English words derived from Arabic—*alcohol, alchemy, algebra*—originally meant *the*, but no one finds "the alcohol" redundant.

I have no good advice on this one. Dropping the *the* runs the risk of sounding pedantic; leaving it in runs the risk of sounding illiterate. Another SKUNKED word, I'm afraid.

HOMOSEXUAL *VERSUS* GAY.

See POLITICALLY LOADED LANGUAGE.

HOPEFULLY.

According to traditionalists, *hopefully* means *in a hopeful way*, not *I hope*. You'll keep them (and me) happy by avoiding *hopefully* in formal writing; use *I hope, we hope, I would like*, or, what's often best of all, leave it out altogether. It's the paradigmatic example of a SKUNKED TERM.

HOUSE STYLE.

Some linguistic questions have no "true" answers, only competing standards used in different places. There are of course differences in spelling and punctuation in various countries, but "house style" refers to the hundreds of choices that each publishing house makes on its own. Newspaper publishers, for instance, often use different rules than book publishers do (see JOURNALISM); lawyers have to follow templates that are common in their profession (see LEGAL WRITING); a press that specializes in software manuals will probably have rules different from those of a publisher that specializes in novels.

Some writers get very uptight about these things—they seethe with rage when someone omits a serial comma, or they crusade passionately for POSSESSIVES in -*s'* rather than -*s's*. But it's not a question of which is "right" or "wrong"; you learn to suit your mechanics to the forum for which you're writing. Save your outrage for things that matter.

Dozens of entries in this guide refer to house styles: see especially APOSTROPHE, CAPITALIZATION, CITATION, COMMAS,

DASH, ELLIPSES, ITALICS, NUMBERS, and PUNCTUATION AND SPACES. See also JOURNALISM, LEGAL WRITING, and SCIENTIFIC WRITING.

HOWEVER.

An irrational fondness for LONG WORDS often leads amateur writers to turn every *but* into a *however*. Don't. A sprinkling of *however*s is fine, but you shouldn't neglect the more straightforward *but*.

When you use it, here's a tip to make your writing livelier: avoid starting your sentences with *however*. This isn't a RULE, just a way to make for better EMPHASIS. This way you save the beginning of the sentence for a more substantial word.

What can you do instead? Starting a sentence with *but* can be a little informal (see BUT AT THE BEGINNING), but it's usually more forceful than starting with *however*. The other possibility is to tuck the *however* inside the sentence: "She did, *however*, finish the book." (You can also try *though*, which is a good way to mix things up when you have too many *however*s.)

Note that this refers only to the CONJUNCTION *however*, not the adverb *however*. "However much he tried, he could never lift it"; "However you did it, it seems to be working again"— they're copacetic.

> Examples:
>
> **Weak:**   However, the papers were delivered on time.
> **Strong:**   But the papers were delivered on time.
>   *or*
>   The papers, however, were delivered on time.

HYPERCORRECTION.

Hypercorrection means being so concerned with getting the grammar right that you get it wrong. For instance, we have it drilled into our heads that "Me and him went to the game" is wrong; it should be "*He and I* went to the game." Too many people end up thinking "He and I" is therefore somehow "more proper," and use it in inappropriate places, like "A message came for he and I"—it should be "A message came for *him and me*." *Whom* is another frequent problem for hypercorrectors; they have the sense that *whom* is somehow more correct than *who*, and use it improperly. But things aren't "more proper" in any abstract sense, only in particular contexts. Try to understand the principles behind the RULES, and you'll make few blunders.

See also AGREEMENT, BETWEEN YOU AND I, and WHOM.

HYPHEN.

A hyphen joins the two parts of a COMPOUND WORD or the two elements of a range: *self-conscious*; pp. 95-97. (Hard-core typography nerds will point out that ranges of numbers are marked with an *en-dash*—if you look carefully at "pp. 95–97," you'll notice that the dash is a little longer than a hyphen and a little shorter than an em-dash—but you needn't worry about it. Type a hyphen.) A compound word used as an adjective is often hyphenated: *a present-tense verb*. (For more details, see PREDICATE.) An exhaustive (not to say exhausting) list of rules and examples appears in *The Chicago Manual of Style*. Don't confuse a hyphen with a DASH, although you can type a dash as two hyphens.

See also -CENTURY.

IBID.

An abbreviation of the LATIN word *ibidem*, meaning "in the same place." It's sometimes used in footnotes or endnotes: "Remember that long citation I gave you in the previous note?—repeat it here." Note that it always means the immediately preceding reference. Since "ibid." is an abbreviation, it usually gets a period at the end, but most house styles suggest roman rather than italics. It was once common, along with "id." (from Latin *idem*, "the same"—not "the same place" but "the same work"). Both are becoming less common, though they hang on in LEGAL WRITING. Unless you're confident your readers will know what you mean, it's wise to be sparing with LATIN ABBREVIATIONS.

-IC AND -ICAL.

Both suffixes are used to produce adjectives, but there's no easy way to tell which is which without looking up the words. Sometimes both the *-ic* an the *-ical* forms exist for the same root with (nearly) the same meaning: *comic* and *comical*, *ironic* and *ironical*, or *electric* and *electrical*. Sometimes both forms exist but with substantially different meanings: *economic* ("related to the economy") and *economical* ("sparing with money" or "giving a good return on an investment"), for instance, or *historic* ("of great importance in history") and *historical* ("related to history" or "set in the past"). Usually, though, only one of the two possibilities is used, and there's no easy way to tell which it is: it's *romantic*, *therapeutic*, *linguistic*, but *hysterical*, *grammatical*, and *rhetorical*. (Note that those adjectives ending in *-ic* often gain an *-al-* when they're turned into adverbs: *romantic* but *romantically*, *automatic* but *automatically*. The only significant exception is *public*, which forms the adverb *publicly*.) Whenever you're in doubt, check a DICTIONARY.

ICON.

The word *icon* comes from Greek, where it means "image," and it became especially strongly identified with pictures of saints and other holy figures. It has become the default name for the little graphical whatchamacallits in computer programs, and there's no reason to object to that. But it's also a CLICHÉ for anything important—James Dean was a cultural icon, Ingmar Bergman a film icon, Elvis Presley a musical icon, and so on. The word is overused; avoid it when you can, looking for something more forceful.

IDIOLECT.

A *language* is shared by a large community: English, for instance, is the first language of most people in the UK, America, Canada, Australia, New Zealand, and much of South Africa, India, and so on. Thing is, the English spoken in Louisiana is pretty far from the English spoken in Cape Town. A *dialect* is a subset of a language shared by a smaller community, often (but not always) regional: Cockney, for instance, is a dialect of English. A dialect is distinguished from a language by a set of departures from the "norm," but these departures are necessarily shared by some community. (I'll let the linguists wrangle over exactly which communities constitute dialects.)

An *idiolect*, on the other hand, is the form of a language spoken by a single person, marked by a set of departures from the "norm" that aren't shared with others, at least not as a package. A person's idiolect constitutes a kind of linguistic fingerprint, since it's by definition unique to an individual. Police forensics folks often look for idiolect markers in, say, ransom letters. It was a series of distinctive verbal tics, for example, that allowed authorities to spot the Unabomber from his "manifesto."

See UNCONSCIOUS HABITS.

IDIOM.

An *idiom* is just a way of expressing something that has been sanctified by long use—often in violation of apparent logic, or at least without any obvious logic behind it.

You can sometimes figure out an idiom from the component words: if I say something is *a dime a dozen*, you can probably figure out that it means "cheap" or "common." Others are impossible to figure out logically. To *kick the bucket* has nothing to do with buckets; if someone *has a screw loose*, it's unlikely the problem will be fixed with a screwdriver.

Even trickier are the more subtle idioms. For instance, in English it's idiomatic to say "I'm going home," even though with every other destination you need a preposition like *to* or *into*: you go *to* work or *into* a store. People learning English often have trouble with this, saying things like "I'm going to home." Even native speakers sometimes get into trouble when they start puzzling over the logic of some phrases, and end up with something that "makes sense" in the abstract, but doesn't conform to general usage: see, for instance, my entry on DOUBLE GENITIVES.

People learning the language often want to ask *why* things are this way; alas, the only answer is, "It just *is*, that's all."

I.E. *VERSUS* E.G.

See E.G. *VERSUS* I.E.

IF *VERSUS* WHETHER.

For many people, the CONJUNCTIONS *if* and *whether* are usually interchangeable: you can say "I wonder whether she'll be home by seven" or "I wonder if she'll be home by seven." Others, though, prefer to use *whether* after verbs of wondering, asking, thinking, and knowing, especially when a finite number of options is implied. In informal settings, you can get away with either, but it never hurts to use *whether* if you suspect your AUDIENCE will bristle at *if*.

Examples:

Disputed: She doesn't know if she'll be able to make it.

I wonder if that brain surgeon knows what he's doing.

Preferred: She doesn't know whether she'll be able to make it.

I wonder whether that brain surgeon knows what he's doing.

IMPACT.

I have to express my distaste here: *impact* should remain a noun; a proposal can *have an impact*, but cannot *impact* anything without degenerating into jargon. Using *impacted* for anything other than a wisdom tooth is inelegant.

IMPERATIVE.

In grammar, an *imperative* is an order: instead of "You *will go*"—the *indicative*—the imperative says: "*Go.*" Instead of "You *will get* the book"—the indicative—the imperative says "*Get the book.*"

It's also sometimes used in other contexts to mean "mandatory" or "necessary." Though the word *imperative* is common in business writing, it's big and ugly and intimidating. Go with *must* or *should*. Instead of the jargony "It is imperative that the forms be completed on time," try "Be sure to complete the forms on time."

IMPLY *VERSUS* INFER.

A speaker *implies* something by hinting at it; a listener *infers* something from what he or she hears. Don't use them interchangeably.

IMPORTANT.

A tip: it's often wise to steer clear of the word *important*, which usually means something like "I think this is relevant, but I haven't a clue how." Especially in crucial parts of your text—say, the first paragraph of a paper, or in the title of an article—you want to be as precise as possible. Some examples of bad thesis statements: "The idea of money is important in Defoe's novels," "The role of honor in the epic poems of ancient Greece is very important," or "Race and gender are very important aspects of Toni Morrison's novels"—they're all close to meaningless. And don't think a SYNONYM like *significant* will save you. Say something PRECISE.

IN BEHALF OF.

See BEHALF.

INCREDIBLE *VERSUS* INCREDULOUS.

An easily CONFUSED PAIR. *Incredible* means "not believable"; *incredulous* means "not believing." A story can be incredible; a person who doubts it can be incredulous.

INDEFINITE ARTICLES.

See ARTICLES.

INDENTING.

The traditional rule for PARAGRAPHS calls for standard line spacing between paragraphs, with the next paragraph slightly indented from the left margin (in typewriter days, it was often five spaces; in the age of proportionally spaced typefaces, it's usually a fixed measurement, say, a quarter or a half of an inch). In business writing, on the other hand, it's common to skip a line between paragraphs and to use no paragraph indenting.

INDEPENDENT CLAUSES.

See DEPENDENT *VERSUS* INDEPENDENT CLAUSES.

INDICATIVE.

See MOOD, SUBJUNCTIVES, and SHALL *VERSUS* WILL.

INDIVIDUAL.

A yucky word, and usually unnecessary. Use *person* or *someone* instead. *Individual* makes sense when you mean to distinguish an individual from a group or corporation, but usually it's just a long way of saying *person*.

INFINITIVE.

The *infinitive* is the form of a verb that doesn't express PERSON, NUMBER, TENSE, or MOOD. It's the "uninflected" form of the verb.

In most English verbs, the present infinitive is the same as the present plural indicative: "we, you, they *listen*," so the infinitive is simply *listen*; "we, you, they *shake*," so the infinitive is *shake*. The verb *to be*, however, is fiercely irregular; the present plural indicative is *are*, but the infinitive is *be*. The infinitive is often marked with the particle *to* (*to listen*, *to shake*, *to be*), though it's not always necessary.

There's also a past infinitive, formed with *have* and the past participle: *to have listened*, *to have shaken*, *to have been*.

See also INFLECTION and SPLIT INFINITIVE.

INFLAMMABLE *VERSUS* FLAMMABLE.

See FLAMMABLE *VERSUS* INFLAMMABLE.

INFLECTION.

Inflection is the process by which words change forms, as when you take the infinitive *to go* and turn it into forms like *go*, *goes*, *going*, *gone*, and so on, when you take a singular noun and make it plural, or when you take an adjective and make it an adverb. Our pronouns change form according to PERSON, NUMBER, and CASE—that is, the function they play in the sentence—producing *I*, *me*, *my*, *mine*.

The "base" form of a VERB is the INFINITIVE. The base form of a NOUN is the singular.

Modern English isn't a very "highly inflected" language—we tack an *s* onto the end of the infinitive to get our third-person singular present verb; we slap *ed* to the end of infinitives to get most of our past tenses; we paste *ing* to the infinitive to get the present participle. With nouns, we add an *s* to most singular nouns to get the PLURALS, apostrophe-*s* for singular POSSESSIVES, and *s*-apostrophe for plural possessives. Our adjectives are inflected only to show COMPARATIVE and superlative forms; ditto our adverbs.

A thousand years ago, OLD ENGLISH was much more highly inflected. We lost most of the inflections in the Middle English period, when word order took over their function. Plenty of languages, though, have more flexibility in word order because they show grammatical relations in their word forms. Those who've studied ancient Greek, Latin, or German will know that every noun and adjective can take dozens of forms. The list of forms an ancient Greek verb can take stretches into the hundreds. On the other hand, many of the East Asian languages are even less inflected than English: Chinese and Vietnamese have hardly any changes in word forms.

INTER *VERSUS* INTRA

Inter means "between"; *intra* means "within." An *interoffice memo* is one going between two (or more) offices; *intramural sports*, though, happen within one campus (*intramural* literally means "within the walls"). Be careful not to confuse them.

INTERESTING.

Sentences beginning "It is interesting that" or "It is significant that" are usually as far from interesting as can be. Don't just state that something is interesting: show it. See also IMPORTANT.

IN TERMS OF.

Often useless padding. Ask yourself whether you can get rid of it.

INTERPOLATION.

Just as you might have to *omit* something from quoted material
with ELLIPSES, you sometimes have to *add* to a quotation to
clarify it. A sentence with only a PRONOUN like *he* or *she*, for
instance, might baffle a reader who doesn't know the context
provided by the surrounding sentences. Or a word or phrase
may need explanation—say, a passage in a foreign language.

In these cases, it's traditional to add material in [square
brackets]. (Newspapers often use parentheses instead of square
brackets, but they're a minority.) Provide an explanation
if the author uses something your audience isn't likely to
understand—"The first words of Joyce's 'Stately, plump Buck
Mulligan' are *Introibo ad altare dei* ['I will go to the altar
of God']." You might need to supply a detail missing in the
original quotation, especially if your reader is likely to be
confused: "As Fairbanks notes, 'The death of three civil rights
workers in Philadelphia [Mississippi] marked a turning point.'"
You might also provide a first name: "It was [George] Eliot's
most successful work." Always the question is whether the
clarification will help your AUDIENCE: there's no need to cram
clarifications and explanations into someone else's writing
unless readers have a real chance of misunderstanding it.

If you're changing a single word or a short phrase, especially
a pronoun, and the word isn't especially interesting in its own
right, it's okay to omit the original and replace it with the
bracketed interpolation: you can change "In that year, after
much deliberation, he issued the Emancipation Proclamation"
to "In [1862], after much deliberation, [Lincoln] issued the
Emancipation Proclamation." If you're hesitant to monkey
with words in the original that may be important—and it's
wise to be circumspect—just add the bracketed interpolation
after the thing you're explaining: "The sixteenth president
[Lincoln] abolished slavery."

You can also use brackets around *part* of a word to indicate
necessary changes in its form. So, for instance, you might
write, "In his brilliant guide to grammar and style, Lynch

provides sage advice on 'us[ing] brackets around *part* of a word.'"

Some HOUSE STYLES call for brackets to indicate changes of upper- and lowercase letters at the beginning of a quotation: "[L]ike this." I don't like it—it clutters a page—but I don't get to make the call, except in things I edit.

Limit square brackets to quotations of others' words. If you need to clarify something in your own prose, use parentheses (as I do here).

See also ELLIPSES and *SIC*.

INTRANSITIVE VERBS.

See TRANSITIVE *VERSUS* INTRANSITIVE VERBS.

INVERTED COMMAS.

See SINGLE QUOTATION MARKS.

IRELAND.

See BRITAIN.

IRONIC.

Resist the impulse to refer to things that are merely coincidental as *ironic*.

Irony is a complicated notion with an even more complicated history. Those with scholarly inclinations should check out Norman Knox's important book, *The Word "Irony" and Its Context, 1500–1755* (Durham: Duke Univ. Press, 1961) and Wayne C. Booth, *A Rhetoric of Irony* (Chicago: Univ. of Chicago Press, 1974). Those without such inclinations should at least be aware that things are messy, and that precision is useful.

Irony usually refers to some kind of gap between what's said and what's meant. The simplest form is *verbal irony*, which in its crudest form is *sarcasm*. If I start praising the infinitely enlightened administrators who run my university, complimenting them for their inexhaustible wisdom and their clarity of expression, most people will recognize that I'm indulging in verbal irony. (The aforementioned bureaucrats won't, but they're beyond hope.)

Other kinds of irony are more complicated. *Dramatic irony* is when a speaker isn't aware of the true meaning of what he or she is saying (as when Sophocles' Oedipus vows he wants to punish the sinner who brought the plague on Thebes, unaware that he's talking about himself). *Socratic irony* describes Socrates' disingenuous pose of ignorance. There are also *situational irony*, *structural irony*, and *romantic irony*. *Cosmic irony* is perhaps the closest to what most people think of as irony: it's when God or fate seems to be manipulating events so as to inspire false hopes, which are inevitably dashed. Thomas Hardy's novels are filled with it. For all of these kinds of irony, the word *ironic* is just dandy.

But you shouldn't use it merely to suggest something coincidental or contrary to expectation. "He thought the plan would make him rich, but it turns out he lost all his money"—that's a pity, but it's not really ironic. Ditto "She spent years looking for her high school sweetheart, but he finally called her a week after she married someone else." Again, a damn shame for all involved—but not really ironic.

A middle ground—sometimes accepted, sometimes not—is for unexpected things that, in the words of *The American Heritage Dictionary*, "suggest…particular lessons about human vanity or folly." Here's their example, which about three-quarters of their usage panel found kosher:

> Ironically, even as the government was fulminating against American policy, American jeans and videocassettes were the hottest items in the stalls of the market.

The idea is that it wasn't merely an unintended consequence; it points up a serious problem of "human inconsistency."

Even though three-quarters of the panel found it acceptable, remember that one in four disagreed, and it hurts to lose such a big chunk of your audience. For that reason, it's always safest to use words like *coincidental, unexpected, improbable,* or *paradoxical* when they're what you mean, and to reserve *ironic* for unambiguous cases of irony.

IRREGARDLESS.

Not a word to be used in respectable company: somewhere between *irrespective* and *regardless.* Use one of these instead.

Is, Is.

Avoid using *is* twice in a row like that. Sometimes it's unambiguously wrong—"The reason is, is that…"—and should be cut for that reason. Sometimes it's technically correct—"What this is is a whatchamacallit"—but it's still clumsy. If you find yourself using *is* twice in a row, revise the sentence to get rid of it.

-ISE AND -IZE.

Many words that end in *-ize* in American English are spelled with *-ise* in BRITISH English (and in much of the Commonwealth): *recognize* (American) and *recognise* (British), *organize* (American) and *organise* (British), and so on. (Some British style guides recommend the *-ize* spellings, but they're in the minority.)

Note, though, that some words *always* get *-ise* on both sides of the Atlantic: *advertise, advise, chastise, circumcise, comprise, compromise, demise, despise, devise, disfranchise, enfranchise, enterprise, excise, exercise, improvise, incise, revise, supervise, surmise, surprise,* and *televise.*

ISSUE.

A terribly vague word, as in "she has issues" or "do you have any issues with this?" It always suggests to me that the writer doesn't have a clear idea of his or her meaning. Look for something more specific and more CONCRETE.

ITALICS.

Use italics for book titles, for EMPHASIS, and for FOREIGN WORDS.

What exactly constitutes a foreign word? It's sometimes unclear whether something has made the transition from the foreign language to English. Consider some words from Yiddish: most people would agree that *mishpocha* (extended family) is still a foreign word, and that *bagel* is now thoroughly naturalized in English. But what about some between the two?—what about *kvetch* or *shlep* or *chutzpah* or *dreck* or *schmatte* or *potch* or *schnorrer*? Cases like this are often judgment calls. Your best bet is to check a DICTIONARY for its verdict. If the word appears in italics, it's probably best to consider it a foreign word and to preserve the italics in your own writing. (Another possibility: if your SPELLING CHECKER doesn't recognize it, it's probably still considered a foreign word. In the list above, *kvetch*, *shlep*, *chutzpah*, and *dreck* all make the cut as English, but my word processor doesn't know *schmatte*, *potch*, or *schnorrer*.)

Be careful, though, not to rely too much on italics for emphasis; they make your writing look amateurish. Let the words do most of the work.

Note that *italics* and <u>underscores</u> "mean" the same thing— typewriters used <u>underscore</u> when italics weren't available—so use one or the other, but not both, in a paper. Publishers working from hard-copy typescripts usually prefer underscores; they're easier for typesetters to catch.

See TITLES and FONTS.

IT CAN BE ARGUED.

Aw, c'mon: *anything* can be argued. Don't pad your writing with useless stuff like this, especially when it's graceless, imprecise, and in the passive voice.

It's *versus* Its.

There's no shortcut; all you can do is memorize the rule. *It's* with an apostrophe means *it is* (or, a little less often and a little less formally, *it has*); *its* without an apostrophe means *belonging to it*. An analogue might provide a mnemonic: think of "he's" ("he is" gets an apostrophe) and "his" ("belonging to him" doesn't).

What about *its'*, with the apostrophe after the *s*?—Never, never, never. Wrong, wrong, wrong. Not in this language, you don't. *Its*, "belonging to it"; *it's*, "it is." That's it.

Jargon.

Jargon is the bane of too much writing—not only academic writing but business English suffers from jargon and technobabble. Of course some technical terms are useful and even necessary, but when I'm in charge, no on will be allowed to abuse the English language with these phrases: *sign off on, re, imperative, impact, methodology, functionality, network, parameters*, etc.

Jews.

See POLITICALLY LOADED LANGUAGE.

Journalism.

Every publisher has its own HOUSE STYLE, but some rules tend to fall into clusters according to the communities they serve. Publishers of SCIENTIFIC WRITING, for instance, differ somewhat among themselves, but as a group they tend to have certain shared preferences for things like citation format, use of the serial comma, and the hyphenation of compound words. Ditto publishers of novels, of art history, of technical specifications, and so on.

It's no surprise, then, that newspapers and magazines have some of their own preferences, areas in which they differ from most book publishers. Some of these differences arose for technological reasons: in the days when setting type meant arranging slugs of lead rather than clicking on icons, many newspapers had no access to italic fonts or square brackets, so they used quotation marks and parentheses instead. Since newspaper columns are narrow, shorter spellings were often used in place of longer ones, serial COMMAS were often omitted, and hyphens were often used in places you wouldn't see in a book. And these habits have become precedents—even now, in the age of computers, newspapers and magazines tend to use the rules they established back in the day.

Many of the rules for newspapers have been picked up elsewhere, especially in business communications. My guess is that many business writers spend more time with newspapers and magazines than with books, and have therefore internalized their rules. No harm there, as long as everything remains consistent.

This entry contains no big surprises. If you're writing for a newspaper or a magazine, you'll probably be expected to follow one set of rules; if you're writing for other forums, you'll probably be expected to follow another. Neither is more "right" than the other.

See also LEGAL WRITING and SCIENTIFIC WRITING.

JUSTIFICATION.

It's better to leave your papers "ragged right" (or "flush left"): don't play with full justification, which introduces big gaps into the lines. See also FONTS.

Language Change

Languages change, and English is no exception. No one has ever succeeded in stopping the process. You can like this fact or you can hate it, but you do have to get used to it.

Vocabulary changes: new words are invented, old words fall out of use, and current words pick up new meanings and lose old ones. Spellings change: a century ago it was common to see *hiccough*; now *hiccup* is much more familiar. Rules about punctuation change: things like the serial comma and the use of other punctuation with a dash are still subjects of disagreement. Even syntax and grammar change: around 1750 the passive progressive—"the book is being printed"—didn't exist; they said "the book is printing." And, much more generally, style changes: what was once considered first-rate prose might strike modern readers as insufferably pompous or wordy.

For some people this is a cause of much fretting; they're convinced that virtually all change is for the worse. (Okay, maybe they're prepared to accept new vocabulary when new inventions demand them, but many people draw the line there.) Some have even gone so far as to call for various ACADEMIES to try to arrest language change.

But it's a losing battle. Even the Académie Française and the Accademia della Crusca haven't managed to change this simple fact of life. If they had succeeded, the French and Italian of 2007 would look an awful lot like the French and Italian of 1707. Trust me: they don't, any more than the English of 2007 looks like the English of 1707.

What to do about it? The first thing is to separate "change" from "decay" in your mind; they're not the same thing. But recognizing change as inevitable doesn't mean you have to embrace every NEOLOGISM that comes along, or that you have to use the ugliest new constructions you hear. There's still plenty of room for TASTE to come into play. If you don't like a new word or usage, don't use it.

This guide, fairly PRESCRIPTIVE as these things go, generally recommends a conservative approach to language change, at least in more FORMAL settings. That's not because change is in itself bad, but because some people in your audience might find newer forms distracting, even offensive. On the other hand, some battles have clearly been lost, and sticking with outdated forms of the language will just make you look pedantic. I always think of Alexander Pope's advice:

> Be not the first by whom the new are tried,
> Nor yet the last to lay the old aside.

Probably a good idea.

LATIN ABBREVIATIONS.

For centuries, Latin was the language of scholarship in the West. It therefore makes sense that we should still have a lot of words, phrases, and abbreviations that come from Latin.

Some general advice: once-common abbreviations like *op. cit.* ("work cited") and phrases like *ex animo* ("from the heart" or "sincerely") are now becoming less common in most scholarly writing, and that's probably a good thing; we have perfectly serviceable English words to make the same point. But a few other Latinisms are holding their own, and you should know what they mean and how to use them. For details, see CF., E.G. *VERSUS* I.E., ETC., IBID., RE, and SIC. Note that whether they should get italics varies from term to term, and often depends on HOUSE STYLE.

LATIN PLURALS.

See PLURALS.

LATINATE *VERSUS* GERMANIC DICTION.

English is an unusual language in that it derives from *two* main language families, Latinate and Germanic. Its origins are Germanic; in the fourth or fifth century, Old English or

Anglo-Saxon was a Germanic dialect, a relative of modern German. (You wouldn't be able to read a word of it without a class in Old English. Here's the first sentence of the most famous Old English poem, *Beowulf*: "Hwæt! We Gardena in geardagum,/Þeodcyninga, þrym gefrunon,/hu ða Æþelingas ellen fremedon." Yes, that's *English*. I warned you.) There was a later influx of Scandinavian words when the Vikings arrived, but the Scandinavian languages are also Germanic, so English remained fundamentally Germanic.

The picture changed some time after 1066, when the Normans—French speakers—invaded England. For a few centuries, the peasants continued to speak a Germanic English while the nobles spoke French (a Romance language, derived from Latin). Over time, though, the two vocabularies began to merge; and where Old English speakers and French speakers had only one word each for something, speakers of the new blended English often had *two*, one based on the Germanic original long used by the peasantry, another based on the French import that had currency in the court. (Later still, a great many words entered the language directly from Latin without stopping along the way at French, and sometimes we have near SYNONYMS from all three origins: *kingly* [related to German *König*], *royal* [from Latin by way of French *roi*], and *regal* [directly from Latin *rex, regis*].)

There's a moral behind this history lesson: even today, nearly a millennium after the Norman Invasion, words often retain CONNOTATIVE traces of their origins. Words of Germanic origin tend to be shorter, more direct, more blunt, while Latinate words tend to be polysyllabic, and are often associated with higher and SCIENTIFIC diction.

The practical lesson: you'll sound more blunt, more straightforward, more forceful, even more forthright, if you draw your words largely from those with Germanic roots. An extensively Latinate vocabulary, on the contrary, suggests a more elevated level of diction. Choose your words carefully, then, with constant attention to your audience and the effects you want to have on them.

LAW.

See LEGAL WRITING.

LAY *VERSUS* LIE.

A frustrating pair. Here's the deal. In the present tense, *lay* is a TRANSITIVE verb, meaning it takes a DIRECT OBJECT: you lay *something* down. *Lie* doesn't take a direct object: something just lies there. If you're tired of holding something, you should *lay it down*; if you're not feeling well, you should *lie down*. (Of course I'm excluding *lie*, "tell an untruth"—this is just the reclining *lie*.)

Not too bad: if this were the whole deal, there'd be nothing to worry about. But it gets messier, because the past tense of *lay* is *laid*, and the past tense of *lie* is, well, *lay*. It's easier in a little table:

	Transitive	Intransitive
Present Tense	He *lays* the bag down.	He *lies* down.
Past Tense	He *laid* the bag down.	He *lay* down.

You can see, then, why it's easy to confuse them. Try to keep them straight: correct usage of *lay* and *lie* is a telling SHIBBOLETH.

LEAD *VERSUS* LED.

Another easily CONFUSED PAIR of words—easily confused because of different and overlapping pronunciations in different situations. Here's what you need to know:

The VERB in the *present tense* (or the INFINITIVE) meaning "to go before" or "to conduct" ("With 85% of the votes counted, Smith leads by a wide margin"; "I promise to lead a good life") is spelled *lead* and pronounced *leed*.

The same verb in the *past tense* ("With 85% of the votes counted, Smith led by a wide margin"; "He led a good life") is spelled *led* and pronounced *led*.

The NOUN meaning "first place" ("She took the lead in the race"), "the biggest part in a play" ("He was angry when his brother got the lead in the school play"), "a leash" ("Keep your dog on a lead"), and "an electrical conductor" ("Connect the lead to the battery") is spelled *lead* and pronounced *leed*.

The noun meaning "the soft, heavy metal used to make bullets" is spelled *lead* and pronounced *led*.

Got that? The only difficult one is the second: the past tense of the verb *to lead* is spelled *led*, not *lead*.

LEGAL WRITING.

Most of the entries in this guide are concerned with writing intended for a general audience—the sort of thing you'd find in most books, newspapers, and magazines, and the same kind of prose you're usually expected to write in college classes and in business. Some communities, though, have their own standards, and if you're writing for one of those communities, you're expected to follow their rules. The legal community is one of them.

I reserve the right to poke fun at lawyers and legal writing from time to time. Many phrases and expressions they use are ugly and clumsy and forbidding to general readers, and I weep when those expressions make their way before a general audience. On the other hand, there are often good reasons for the seeming fussiness of legal writing: decades of case history have determined that certain verbal formulas have certain precise meanings, and people who draw up contracts or other legal deeds have to use their language with great care.

I don't begrudge the lawyers their dense jargon when they're writing documents that may be fought over in court: if they want to use AND/OR, THEREFOR, MONIES, and more LATIN abbreviations than you can find in a classical dictionary, that's their prerogative. But it's usually best to avoid legalese in other kinds of writing. You can emulate a legal writer's passion for precision, but don't assume that mindlessly throwing around words like *aforementioned* or *whereat* actually contributes to readability.

See also JOURNALISM and SCIENTIFIC WRITING.

LEND *VERSUS* LOAN.

Some people are bothered by the word *loan* as a VERB, preferring to use *lend* in its place. There's not much reason for the anxiety—*loan* has been a verb since around the year 1200, and I think an eight-hundred-year probation is long enough for anyone—but it's now little used in Britain. It thrives, though, in America. My advice: don't be bothered by *loan* as a verb but, if you want to avoid irritating those who have this hangup, it's never wrong to use *lend*.

LESS *VERSUS* FEWER.

See FEWER *VERSUS* LESS.

LIAISE.

The VERB *liaise*—a BACK-FORMATION from the NOUN *liaison*—is now pretty common in British usage. In America, though, it's still considered kinda JARGONY, common in business but not particularly elegant or GRACEFUL. I recommend you avoid it.

LIFESTYLE.

A yucky word that has no clear meaning associated with it. It comes out of 1920s psychoanalysis, but it's been co-opted and turned into a vague, vogue word to refer to character, habits, beliefs, and such. Because it's so nebulous, and because it smacks so much of the twentieth century, it's best avoided in English papers. (I'd say it's best avoided *everywhere*, but my authority extends only so far.) Try to find something more precise: what exactly do you mean when you talk about someone's *lifestyle*?

LIGATURES.

The word *ligature* refers to things that are tied or bound together—in this case, combinations of letters that are printed as a single character, like œ or æ.

A few ligatures are part of the (traditional) spelling of some words: the œ in *phœnix*, for instance, or the æ in *archæology*. Others don't affect the spelling, but do affect the appearance of words on the page: in many professionally typeset books, you'll notice that *ff*, *fl*, *fi*, *ffl*, and *ffi* are not separate letters, but joined together into a single character. (Some older typefaces did the same with *ct* and *st*, though these are exceedingly rare today.)

Most words that once had ligatures as part of their spelling have now dropped them, usually printing the original combinations as separate letters (*phoenix*, *archaeology*), but sometimes, especially in America, reducing the spelling to a simple *e* (older British spellings like *œconomics* and *mediæval* are examples). In most cases you should use the modern spellings, lest you seem eccentrically old-fashioned. *Curriculum vitæ* looks downright quaint in the twenty-first century.

When you're quoting published material, on the other hand, you should carefully preserve the ligatures that are actually part of the spelling. If your source writes *Julius Cæsar* or *Œdipus*, so should you; if you're quoting an older version of the reference work from when it was called the *Encyclopædia Britannica*, you should follow your source exactly. You don't have to worry about the other ligatures—things like *ct*, *st*, *ff*, and so on—since they're the responsibility of the publisher.

LIKE.

I trust I needn't comment on the ignorant, slack-jawed habit of using *like* as a verbal crutch: "It was just, like, y'know, like, really weird." (Actual sentence overheard on the New York City subway: "He was just like—*pf!*, and I was all like, whatever.") It's bad enough in speech: I encourage people to try to go an entire day without saying *like*, and few can manage. If you use it in writing, though, you should be afflicted with plagues and boils. Shame on you.

LIKE *VERSUS* AS.

See AS *VERSUS* LIKE.

LINKING VERBS.

English VERBS come in several varieties. Most are ACTION VERBS, those that describe something that *happens*: think of *hit, run, read, shoot, sleep*, even *prognosticate*. These action verbs can be either TRANSITIVE OR INTRANSITIVE, depending on whether or not they take a DIRECT OBJECT: you can *read a book*, so *read* is a transitive verb; you just *sleep*, no direct object, so it's an intransitive verb.

Linking verbs, on the other hand, don't describe something that happens; instead, they say the subject and the PREDICATE of a clause are linked in some way. The most obvious are *verbs of being*: *is, are, were*, and so on. But there are also verbs like *look, sound, smell, feel, seem*, and *appear*, all of which describe not an action but a state of being. When you say "She looks tired," you're linking the subject, *she*, with the predicate, *tired*, and essentially saying "She *is* tired"; when you say "It sounds right," you're linking *it* with *right*, and essentially saying "It *is* right." (The links can also be negative: "That doesn't seem right," or "He never sounds angry.")

There are two things important to remember about linking verbs:

> First, they can never be PASSIVE: only TRANSITIVE verbs can be passive, and linking verbs are never transitive.

> Second, since they're linking the subject with the predicate, the predicate has to be either a NOUN PHRASE or what's called a "predicate adjective," but not an adverb.

This point about predicate adjectives instead of adverbs will be clearer in some examples:

"It smells very *bad*" (adjective), not "It smells very *badly*" (adverb). You're really saying "The sense of smell tells me it *is* bad."

"The music sounds *great*" (adjective), not "The music sounds *greatly*" (adverb). You're really saying "The sense of sound tells me it *is* great."

Just to keep you on your toes, many words that serve as linking verbs can also be action verbs. *Smell*, for instance, can mean both "give off an odor" (linking verb) and "sniff" (action verb). *Look* can mean both "appear" (linking verb) and "peer out" (action verb). When it's an action verb, it *does* take an adverb, not an adjective. If you're talking about someone applying to be a professional perfume tester who doesn't know how to use his sense of smell, I suppose you'd say he *smells badly*—he can't sniff well. But that's an obscure possibility, and usually you mean "smells *bad*," not "*badly*"; "looks *happy*," not "looks *happily*."

And to keep you not merely on your toes but on your tippy-toes, some things that look like adverbs actually function as adjectives. The most important is *well*, which is usually an adverb ("Sarah handled the interview well"), but which can also be an adjective when it refers to health: "Because Tom still wasn't feeling well, he decided to sleep in."

It sounds confusing, and I suppose it is. Try to remember, though, that if the verb is implying that the subject *is* something (rather than *does* something), then you probably want an adjective, not an adverb: "The idea *sounds good*"; "She *looks drunk*"; "The month-old Chinese food in the back of the fridge *smells terrible*."

Examples:

Wrong: I couldn't make it to work because I was feeling very badly.

Right: I couldn't make it to work because I was feeling very bad.

LISTING.

Don't use *listing* as a noun where *list* will do. A phone book is a *list* of names and numbers, each of which is a *listing*.

LISTS.

See ABOVE, THE FOLLOWING, ASYNDETON AND POLYSYNDETON, and COMMAS.

LITANY.

Litany originally referred to a form of prayer, something repeated according to a formula. It's now widely used to mean any kind of list, especially a list of bad things—a litany of complaints, a litany of failures, a litany of horrors, a litany of half-truths. I have no principled objection to this more expansive use, but it is a CLICHÉ; use it sparingly.

LITERALLY.

Use the word *literally* with care, and only where what you are saying is *literally* true. "We were *literally* flooded with work" is wrong because the *flood* is a metaphorical one, not an actual deluge. Don't use *literally* where *really*, *very*, or *extremely* will do. For that matter, you can often lose the adverb altogether with no loss of force or precision. (For more on metaphor, see MIXED METAPHORS.)

Examples:

Weak: He literally exploded with rage.
Strong: He exploded with rage.

LOATH *VERSUS* LOATHE.

Although they come from the same root and they're both related to dislike, they're not the same. *Loath* (with the *th* unvoiced, as in *thin*) is an ADJECTIVE; it means "reluctant" or "unwilling": *I'm loath to comment on it.* (It's also sometimes spelled *loth*, though that's rare.) *Loathe* (with the *th* voiced, as in *this*) is a VERB; it means "hate" or "abhor": *I loathe that sorry*

S.O.B. There's also an adjective, *loathsome*, meaning "hateful" or "repulsive."

LONG WORDS.

There's nothing inherently wrong with long words, but too many people think a long word is always better than a short one. It doubtless comes from a desire to impress, to sound more authoritative, but it usually ends in IMPRECISION and GRACELESSNESS—and, what may be worse, if you use long words improperly you sound like an ass. (Look up *malapropism* in your DICTIONARY or, better yet, read Richard Brinsley Sheridan's play, *The Rivals*.) Words like FUNCTIONALITY and METHODOLOGY have their proper uses, but they're not the same as *function* and *method*. See also ANTICIPATE, UTILIZE, OBFUSCATION, and VOCABULARY.

LOOSE *VERSUS* LOSE.

The VERB *to lose*—one *o*—means "to mislay" (you can *lose* your keys or *lose* your mind); it's also the opposite of *to win*. It's past tense is *lost*. *Loose*—two *o*'s—is usually an ADJECTIVE, but it can also be a verb, and it's easy to confuse it with *lose*. The verb *to loose* means "to release" or "to let free"; it can also mean "to undo" or "to make loose." Its past tense is *loosed*. The pronunciations are also different: *to lose* ends in a *z* sound; *to loose* ends in a clear *s* sound.

Man.

It was once very common to use the word *man* to refer to all humankind, not just males, but the habit is in decline. Just as well. You lose nothing by opting for *humanity* or something similar, and you avoid the risk of confusion. See POLITICALLY LOADED LANGUAGE.

Massive.

An absurdly overused CLICHÉ. There's no logical reason not to treat *massive* or *massively* metaphorically; the problem is that it seems to be our age's only intensifier.

In a single day's news I read about "a massive nationwide manhunt," "massive civilian casualties," a "massive lead in the race," a "massive height advantage," "a massive systems failure," a "massive tourism injection," "massive corruption," "massive goodwill," "massive devastation outside the Australian embassy" prompting a "massive security increase," "massive car-bombings" and a "massive hurricane" each prompting "massive evacuations," a "massive recall," a "massive crisis that hit the airline industry," and the president's "massive failure."

Can we please look for something a little more creative?

May *versus* Can.

See CAN *VERSUS* MAY.

Maybe *versus* May Be.

The word *maybe* grew out of the two separate words *may be*, but the two forms now have different applications. The one-word *maybe* is an adverb meaning "perhaps" or "possibly": "Maybe it'll rain." In other cases you need to keep the two words separate: "This may be the most boring book I've ever read."

MECHANICS.

The niggling technical details of writing—spelling, punctuation, indenting, double spacing, all that sort of thing—are known as *mechanics*. Amateur writers often think they're above such trivialities; pros realize that sloppiness always lowers them in the eyes of their AUDIENCE.

MEDIA.

According to the purists, *media* a PLURAL noun: print is a medium, radio is a medium, television is a medium; together they are media. Therefore "the media *are*" is preferable to "the media *is*." The word is increasingly being used in the singular, but there are still enough holdouts to warrant some care. See AGREEMENT and DATA.

METHODOLOGY.

A *methodology* is a study of, or a system of, *methods*. Usually you mean *method* instead of *methodology*. Like FUNCTIONALITY, *methodology* is a favorite of longwordophiles.

MICROSOFT WORD.

MS Word, in its many versions, is now the most common word processor on both the PC and the Macintosh. It's so widespread that it deserves a special note. The "AutoCorrect" feature, in particular, can cause problems. It was designed by and for people who like high-tech toys, not by and for people who write.

An incomplete list of the hassles:

The auto-correction of spelling might be okay for memos, but it can be disastrous for English papers, especially if you're writing about anything more than a few decades old. When you're quoting a work, you have to follow the spelling and capitalization exactly. Don't let your word processor "fix" what ain't broke.

Word wants to make the letters that accompany ordinal numbers—the *st* in first, the *nd* in second, the *rd* in third, and the *th* in other numbers—superscripts: not 11th, but 11th. Humbug. Look around: you'll notice that no professionally printed books use superscripts, and neither should you. Besides, most HOUSE STYLES say most ordinal numbers should be spelled out: *eleventh.*

Word turns straight quotation marks into curly ones (they call them "smart quotes," but I remain skeptical about the intelligence of the operation). No serious problem there, except that the curly quotation marks can be difficult to transmit electronically (they're not part of the standard ASCII code). But Word also plays with APOSTROPHES, turning them into paired single quotation marks (also known as "inverted commas"), and it often makes a mess of it. Worst is Word's habit of turning *initial* apostrophes into open single quotation marks. When you refer to decades with an initial apostrophe, it should be '60s (apostrophe), not '60s (open single quote), but Word doesn't care. Ditto some mostly obsolete words like *'tis*: apostrophe, not open single quotation mark as in *'tis.*

Solutions? For starters, turn off the superscript ordinals; there's no reason for them in the world. (It's under "Tools," at least in the current versions of Word.) You can also turn off the "smart quotes," but if you prefer to keep them, you can force an apostrophe that goes the right way by typing two apostrophes—one will automatically be open, the other close—and then deleting the first one.

See also SPELLING CHECKERS and GRAMMAR CHECKERS for comments on how word processors' attempts to be helpful can get in the way of good writing.

MIGHT COULD.

An idiom in some of the informal varieties of American English, but not STANDARD ENGLISH, and therefore not suitable for FORMAL writing.

MIXED METAPHOR.

In a *metaphor*, one thing is likened to another—whether my love to a red, red rose, or the thing that supports a tabletop to a leg. Vivid and thought-provoking metaphors are called "living": when Homer likens the sunlight at dawn to rosy fingers, he invokes an unexpected image. Over time, though, many once-living metaphors become old hat, and by the time they've simply become the usual way to refer to something— the lip of a jug, the eye of a needle—they're called "dead." Of course many fall between the two classes.

(A digression: some distinguish *metaphor* from *simile*, insisting that a metaphor is *implicit*, whereas a simile *explicitly* likens one thing to another with "like" or "as." Others treat simile as a *kind* of metaphor, one that happens to use "like" or "as." I'm easy.)

A vivid metaphorical imagination is a sign of a good writer; a bad one is a sign of a bad writer. Here's the danger: it's possible to use metaphors badly without knowing you're using metaphors at all, because they're far more common than we realize. The secret is to pay attention to those between living and dead (we might call them "moribund"). If we forget that they're metaphors, they can become hopelessly scrambled. Consider this sentence, a more or less realistic example of business writing:

> We were swamped with a shocking barrage of work, and the extra burden had a clear impact on our workflow.

Let's count the metaphors: we have images of a marsh (*swamped*), electrocution or striking (*shocking*), a military assault (*barrage*), weight (*burden*), translucency (*clear*), a physical impression (*impact*), and a river (*flow*), all in a mere twenty words. If you can summon up a coherent mental image including all these elements, your imagination's far superior to mine.

That was a made-up example; here's a real one, from *The New York Times*, 11 June 2001:

Over all, many experts conclude, advanced climate research in the United States is fragmented among an alphabet soup of agencies, strained by inadequate computing power and starved for the basic measurements of real-world conditions that are needed to improve simulations.

Let's see: research is fragmented among soup (*among*?); it is strained (you can strain soup, I suppose, but I'm unsure how to strain research); and it is starved—not enough soup, I guess. Or maybe the soup has been strained too thoroughly, leaving just the broth. I dunno.

It's not just journalists who make blunders like this. Joseph Addison, one of the most important writers of the eighteenth century, included these lines in his *Letter from Italy*:

I bridle in my struggling Muse with pain,
That longs to launch into a nobler strain.

The critic Samuel Johnson took him to task in his *Lives of the Poets*:

To *bridle* a *goddess* is no very delicate idea: but why must she be *bridled*? because she *longs to launch*; an act which was never hindered by a *bridle*: and whither will she *launch*? into a *nobler strain*. She is in the first line a *horse*, in the second a *boat*; and the care of the poet is to keep his *horse* or his *boat* from *singing*.

This doesn't mean metaphors can *never* be mixed. Sometimes they're good for comic effect. Sometimes they make for vivid characterization: Hamlet has a famous one, when he considers whether he should "take arms against a sea of troubles"—arm yourself all you like; the sea doesn't care—but it's dramatically effective. Most of the time, though, mixed metaphors show a writer not in control of his or her material.

The moral of the story: pay attention to the literal meaning of figures of speech and your writing will come alive.

Don't, by the way, confuse mixed metaphors with mangled CLICHÉS—though a mixed metaphor *might* result from a botched cliché, they're not the same thing. If there's no metaphor, there's no mixed metaphor.

MODIFIER.

A modifier simply gives additional information about a word: instead of "bench"—any old bench—we get "*wooden* bench"; instead of "read"—read *how?*—we get "read *quickly.*" Modifiers are usually ADJECTIVES OR ADVERBS.

MOMENTARILY.

Traditionally, *momentarily* meant *for a moment*, not *in a moment*. The battle may be lost by now, but I confess I still get antsy when I hear things like "We'll be taking off momentarily." Besides, if you mean soon, why not save four syllables and say "soon"?

MONIES.

Outside LEGAL WRITING, it's best to treat *money* as a mass noun, which therefore never takes a PLURAL. See COUNT VERSUS MASS NOUNS.

MOOD.

Mood is a property of VERBS that's a little difficult to describe, because we don't always indicate moods with INFLECTIONS in English. Here's what the *American Heritage Dictionary* has to say:

> A verb form or a set of verb forms inflected to indicate the manner in which the action or state expressed by a verb is viewed with respect to such functions as factuality, possibility, or command.

The most familiar mood is the *indicative*: it *indicates* that something has happened, is happening, or will happen. I've never done a systematic survey, but I'd guess that a large majority of clauses spoken or written in English are indicative.

Another mood we have in English is the IMPERATIVE, which gives an order. "You'll get out of here" is the indicative; it

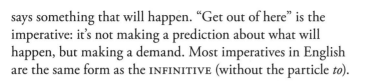

says something that will happen. "Get out of here" is the imperative: it's not making a prediction about what will happen, but making a demand. Most imperatives in English are the same form as the INFINITIVE (without the particle *to*).

There's also the SUBJUNCTIVE mood, which marks a "contingent or hypothetical action" (*American Heritage Dictionary* again). Compared to many other languages (and even compared to earlier versions of English), modern English doesn't do much with subjunctives; it probably won't be long before they're completely gone. But they're still occasionally used in cases that are conditional or contrary to fact.

MOOT QUESTION.

Moot is one of those odd words that can mean opposite things. Traditionally a *moot question* was one that could be debated; today, especially in America, it usually means a question that's not worth debating. Both meanings, though, are still in circulation, so you should use the word with care, especially with an international audience. Be certain your meaning is clear.

MORE SO.

Two words, not one.

Moslem *versus* Muslim.

Arabic uses a different alphabet from ours, and there are different ways of TRANSLITERATING Arabic words into English. *Moslem* and *Muslim* are two different ways of spelling the same Arabic word, and for a long time *Moslem* was the standard way of writing the word in our alphabet. The problem is that the English or American pronunciation of *Moslem* is, by coincidence, close to the Arabic pronunciation of another word for "oppressor." So *Moslem* has been losing ground, and most newspapers, magazines, and scholarly journals now prefer *Muslim*. I suggest you do the same.

A very old-fashioned term was *Mohammedan* or *Mahometan*, though they've been out of use for decades. Even older terms, now out of favor, include *Mussulman* and *Musselman*. Avoid them.

See POLITICALLY LOADED LANGUAGE.

Ms.

The use of *Ms.* (often without the final period, *Ms*) in place of either *Mrs.* or *Miss*—in other words, as a title for a woman that makes no reference to her marital status—was controversial for a long time. Through the 1970s and '80s many politically active feminists argued for it, and many people at the other end of the political spectrum resolved not to use it because they resented the politics of those who did.

(The title didn't originally come out of the feminist movement; it was suggested as long ago as the early 1950s, and began picking up adherents in the early '60s. It really caught on, though, after Gloria Steinem founded *Ms. Magazine* in 1971.)

Whatever your take on the politics, plenty of time has passed since the early '70s. By now even most culturally conservative publications have recognized that it's convenient to have a title that you can apply to any woman without having to do research on whether she's married. It's now the default way to refer to women, in the same way *Mr.* is the default way to refer to a man.

One useful caution comes up in the usage note in the *American Heritage Dictionary*: "Some women prefer *Miss* or *Mrs.*, however, and courtesy requires that their wishes be respected." Good advice, I think. See POLITICALLY LOADED LANGUAGE.

MUSLIM.

See MOSLEM *VERSUS* MUSLIM.

MYSELF.

As a reflexive PRONOUN ("I cut myself") or an intensifier ("I did it myself"), the word is fine. But a romance with the LONG WORD often leads people to use *myself* where *I* or *me* is preferable: "The work was completed by Pat and myself," for instance. My guess is that eighty-three percent of *myself*s in business writing could safely disappear and no one would miss them.

Note that it's always one word—*myself*, not *my self*—as are the other compounds with *self*, including *yourself*, *himself*, *herself*, *itself*, *oneself*, and (in the plural) *yourselves* and *themselves*. (There's no *theirself* or *theirselves*; you'll see *themself* only with the singular *they*, for which see the entry on SEXIST LANGUAGE AND THE INDEFINITE THIRD PERSON.)

NAMES.

The usual rule for writing personal names is to give the full name on the first appearance in your text; after that first reference, you give just the family name (usually the last name). In other words: on first reference, "Alan Greenspan"; thereafter, simply "Greenspan"; on first reference, "Jane Austen"; thereafter, simply "Austen"; on first reference, "Mao Zedong"; thereafter, simply "Mao."

In a familiar essay, especially when you're dealing with friends and family members, it's okay to stick with the first name—your cousin Janet Rogers can be plain old Janet. In such cases you can even use a nickname. But when you're dealing with a public figure—a politician, a writer, a historical figure—stick with the family name.

There are, inevitably, exceptions. When you're talking about several members of the same family, or anyone who shares a name, you may need to use first names. In a comparison of novels by Emily Brontë and Charlotte Brontë, it makes sense to refer to "Emily" and "Charlotte"; if you're talking about the Shelleys, you'll probably find it easiest to refer to "Percy" and "Mary."

Many ancient and medieval authors don't have given and family names as we understand them, and they require special handling. Most Greek authors go by a single name—Homer, Herodotus, Aristotle—and, although most Latin names come in three parts, we usually use just one of the names (sometimes in a slightly modified form) to refer to them: Marcus Tullius Cicero is known as Cicero, and Publius Ovidius Naso is known as Ovid. Many medieval European authors had only a given name, or sometimes a given name with a description: Julian of Norwich was named Julian and came from Norwich; Andreas Capellanus was Andreas, the chaplain. When you refer to these people, after giving the full name you use just "Julian" or "Andreas."

Even some modern names can be tricky. Most cultures put the given name before the family name, but not all, so you have to know which part is the family name and which the given one. The proper way to refer to Mao Zedong is "Mao," not "Zedong": in China the usual practice is to put the family name before the given names. Most Icelandic names consist only of a given name and a "patronymic," or a version of the father's name; the proper way to refer to the Icelandic novelist Arnaldur Indriðason is with the full version on the first reference, and then simply "Arnaldur" thereafter. (The "ð" is an Icelandic letter, the "eth," pronounced "th.")

Titles (Mr., Ms., Dr., Sir, Lord, Baron, Duchess) can be a bear. There's usually no need to give titles that come *after* the full names—things like Ph.D., M.S., and so on—unless there's some specific reason to highlight the credentials. Titles that come *before* the full names are more complicated. Some HOUSE STYLES use courtesy titles (Ms., Dr., Prof.) on every appearance: the *New York Times*, for instance, always refers to everyone by full name on the first appearance, and then as "Mr. Smith" or "Ms. Jones" thereafter, at least with living people. In academic writing, though, it's much more common to give just the last name with no titles at all. (Besides, it would look downright silly to talk about "Mr. Plato.")

Nobles and other honorific titles present their own set of challenges. Kings and Queens go by their given names; the current Queen of England is "Queen Elizabeth II" on first reference and "Elizabeth" thereafter. Knights of the realm are often referred to by "Sir" and a given name: "Sir Roger Bannister" on the first appearance; "Sir Roger" thereafter. The hereditary nobility and life peers are usually referred to not by their family name but their titles: Ralph George Algernon Percy, 12th Duke of Northumberland, would be called "Northumberland," not "Percy." (Nifty little bit of trivia: the family seat of the Northumberlands is Alnwick Castle, pronounced "Annick"; it was used for many of the exterior shots of Hogwarts Academy in the Harry Potter films.) But every culture has its own rules on things like this, and the number of possibilities is staggering. If ever you find yourself traveling in the social circles where you need to get these things right, order yourself a copy of *Debrett's Correct Form* (many editions) to avoid an embarrassing faux pas.

Once upon a time it was common to use "Miss" or "Mrs." with every female writer's name, even when there was no corresponding "Mr." for the men. Here, for instance, is part of the table of contents of Austin Dobson's *Handbook of English Literature* (1897): "Byron.—Shelley.—Keats.—Leigh Hunt, Landor.—Other Poets.—The Novelists: Mrs. Radcliffe.— Lewis, Godwin.—Miss Edgeworth, Miss Austen.—Scott." Notice all the men get just last names (except for Leigh Hunt, so as not to confuse him with his brother John); notice, too, that all the women are identified by title. That practice is pretty thoroughly abandoned, and good riddance; it's an embarrassing double standard.

It was once common, especially in the United Kingdom, to refer to given names as "Christian names" (apparently from the practice of officially giving a child his or her name at the time of baptism, or "christening"). That has fallen out of favor in most situations; in an increasingly multicultural world, remember that Moishe, Mohammed, and Mohan may be amused or may be offended by references to their "Christian names." Unless you can be certain no one in your AUDIENCE will object, go with something less controversial.

NATIONALITY.

Americans have a habit, baffling to the rest of the English-speaking world, of using *nationality* to refer to ethnic groups. When I was growing up, many told me my "nationality" was Irish, even though I was born and bred in the United States, and have spent a total of a week in the Republic of Ireland. My *ethnicity* is indeed Irish, since most of my ancestors came from there, but my *nationality* is American.

NATURE.

No offense to the ecologists, but *nature* is often useless. *Decisions of a delicate nature* would be better if they were just plain old *delicate decisions.*

NAUSEOUS.

Ask an old-timer, and he'll tell you that *nauseous* means *causing* nausea, not *suffering from* it. The word for the latter is *nauseated.* A decaying carcass is *nauseous*, and (unless you go for such things) will probably make you *nauseated.*

NECESSITATE.

Ugly business jargon. If you mean *require,* say *require* or rework the sentence so that *necessitate* is not necessitated.

NEOLOGISMS.

Greek *neo,* "new," and *logos,* "word": new words. (The accent is on the second syllable: "nee-AH-lo-jiz-ms.") They come about by various means. Here are some of the ways new words enter a language.

Some are imported from other languages: when English speakers encountered a round breadroll with a hole in it popular among Jews, they simply borrowed the Yiddish word *beygel* (adapting the spelling to *bagel*); a Muslim holy war against infidels is a *jihad*, from the Arabic. (Paying attention to the words we borrow from different languages at different times can tell us a lot about our attitudes toward their cultures.) Note, though, that their meanings in English may be different from their meanings in their original languages: Latin *video* means "I see," whereas it's come to be a noun related to technologies used to reproduce moving images. The prefix *cyber* comes from Greek *kybernan,* "to steer, to govern," and has a long and complicated history before it comes to mean "vaguely related to computers."

Some phrases are translated, piece by piece, from another language. These are called *calques*: examples are *marriage of convenience*, translated literally from the French *mariage de convenance*, and *superman*, from the German *Übermensch*. (Sometimes the loans go the other way: English *hotdog* shows up in Québécois French as *le chien chaud*.)

Some come about when an old word gets a new prefix or suffix. Horace Walpole made up heaps of words: he took an old name for Sri Lanka, *Serendip*, and added a suffix to get *serendipity*, "the faculty of making happy and unexpected discoveries by accident," because a fairy-tale called *The Three Princes of Serendip* included many such discoveries. He turned a put-down aimed at a person into a general term for stupidity with *nincompoophood*. Many of Walpole's neologisms were similarly facetious: for "greenness" and "blueness" he coined *greenth* and *blueth*. When he wanted a word meaning "intermediateness," he made up *betweenity*.

Many are made by combining familiar words or roots to make new combinations. When in the early twentieth century inventors created a new doohickey that let them transmit moving pictures over long distances, they had no word for it. So they took the Greek word *tele*, meaning "at a distance," and the Latin word *visio*, "sight," and came up with *television*. (They had to pair Greek and Latin—usually a no-no—because the combination of the two Greek words—*tele*, "far," and *skopeo*, "see"—was already used for a different kind of "far-seeing" technology, the telescope.) In 1990, a writer for the *Village Voice* coined an adjective to describe a straight person "experimenting" with homosexuality, and made up *bi-curious*.

A special kind of combination of familiar words is the *portmanteau word*—a term made up by Humpty Dumpty in Lewis Carroll's *Through the Looking-Glass*. Carroll himself made up a bundle of them in "Jabberwocky": *slithy*, for instance, combines *slimy* with *lithe*. Others are more familiar: a *motel* is a "motor-hotel"; *smog* is a combination of smoke and fog. Snoop Dogg made up *bootylicious* in 1992.

Some words began life as ACRONYMS or other abbreviations: *laser* is an abbreviation of "light amplification by stimulated emission of radiation"; *AIDS* is "Acquired Immune Deficiency

Syndrome"; a *nimby* is someone who doesn't want development in his or her neighborhood, from "not in my back yard." (New acronyms tend to get all caps; if they stick around, they sometimes get demoted to lowercase letters.) Note, though, that the habit of forming words from initial letters didn't get going in earnest until the twentieth century, and many stories that derive familiar words from abbreviated phrases are bogus.

Other kinds of abbreviation occasionally make new words: the noun *weblog* (itself a neologism in 1997) got clipped to *blog* in 1999, and quickly turned into a verb and an adjective as well.

Some come from BACK-FORMATIONS, when a root word is abbreviated under the mistaken impression that it's a COMPOUND WORD.

A small number of new words are almost pulled out of thin air. Computerfolk borrowed the word *grok*—"to understand profoundly"—from Robert A. Heinlein's novel *Stranger in a Strange Land*: it's not from Latin, Greek, or German, but from the Martian language. The problem with these is that outsiders can rarely guess the meaning, so they rarely flourish.

A few things to note about neologisms. Remember, all words were once necessarily neologisms; they all had to be new to English at one time or another. Bear this in mind before you make any sweeping pronouncements about them. Individual neologisms might be good or bad, useful or useless, clever or dimwitted, appealing or ugly as sin—but there's nothing "improper" about them in principle, whatever you think of particular examples.

Coining your own neologisms requires caution. First, you have to be certain your audience will understand their meaning; second, you have to be sure readers won't be distracted—that is, annoyed—by the novelty or informality. Too often neologisms are ugly and graceless: things like *rearchitecturing*, *foundherentism*, and *to repristinate*. It's therefore wise to ask yourself whether there's already a good word in the language that does the job.

It's hard to offer a prognosis on the lifespan of a neologism. Some stick around and become part of the standard language; others blossom, flourish, and die in a few years; others still are meant to be used only once (they're called *nonce words*). It's a safe bet Walpole didn't expect *greenth* would be widespread; he was simply playing with the language. (James Joyce's *Finnegans Wake* is filled to bursting with nonce words.)

"Never" and "Always."

Any grammatical or stylistic RULE beginning with "Never" or "Always" should be suspect, and that includes the ones in this guide. No word or construction in the language is *completely* valueless (even if some come pretty close). Apply all guidelines intelligently and sensitively, and forsake pedantic BUGBEARS in favor of GRACE. See AUDIENCE and read it twice.

Newspapers.

See JOURNALISM.

Next [Monday, Tuesday,…].

Some people use the phrase "next Monday" to refer to "the very next Monday to come"; others use it to mean "the Monday *after* the one that's about to come" or "the Monday of next week." There's no "right" choice—just be aware that readers may have different ideas of what you mean. If you need to be precise, spell out the date.

Nor.

Although there are other possibilities, you can't go wrong if you use *nor* only after the word *neither*: instead of "Keats did not write novels nor essays," use either "Keats did not write novels *or* essays" or "Keats wrote *neither* novels *nor* essays." (You *can*, however, say "Keats did not write novels, nor did he write essays.")

NORMAL.

Use *normal* with care: it can carry the neutral meaning of "like the majority," but it can also carry a more judgmental meaning in which being abnormal is tantamount to being wrong. Be careful about labeling things *normal* or *abnormal*; your readers may miss your meaning, and may even take offense.

See POLITICALLY LOADED LANGUAGE.

NORMALCY.

The traditional word is *normality*. President Warren G. Harding famously used *normalcy* in a speech in 1920, calling for "a return to normalcy" after the Great War. (Harding didn't make it up; it first showed up in English in 1857. But it was never common, and Harding seems to have coined it anew. He certainly gave it new currency.)

Now, Harding was no inspiring speaker; William McAdoo commented, "His speeches left the impression of an army of pompous phrases moving over the landscape in search of an idea." H. L. Mencken was even more forceful:

> He writes the worst English that I have ever encountered. It reminds me of a string of wet sponges; it reminds me of tattered washing on the line; it reminds me of stale bean soup, of college yells, of dogs barking idiotically through endless nights. It is so bad that a sort of grandeur creeps into it. It drags itself out of the dark abysm of pish, and crawls insanely up the topmost pinnacle of posh. It is rumble and bumble. It is flap and doodle. It is balder and dash.

Some people have therefore been knocking *normalcy* as a semiliterate barbarism ever since.

The masses, though, don't give a hoot about Mencken's concerns, and probably don't even remember we ever *had* a president called Harding. *Normalcy* has become ever more common since. Most usage guides now consider it STANDARD ENGLISH; some even suggest it's preferable to *normality*.

My advice? There's no point in fulminating over the word; it's probably here to stay. On the other hand, enough people dislike the word that it's probably wise to avoid it in your own writing.

NOT UN-.

This phrase, as in "The subtleties did not go unnoticed," is often an affectation. Be more direct.

NOUN.

A noun, as the "Schoolhouse Rock" song would have it, is a person, a place, or a thing. Piece o' cake.

Well, a *qualified* piece o' cake. We have to define *thing* broadly enough to include things that aren't particularly thingy. *Heat* is a noun; *January* is a noun; *innovation* is a noun; *asperity* is a noun.

Linguists use the term *noun phrase* to refer to any word or group of words that's used as a noun: *his far-seeing eye*, for instance, is a single noun phrase, even though it's made up of a possessive pronoun (*his*), an adverb (*far*), a participial verb (*seeing*), and a noun (*eye*). I've disavowed any intention of using the terms of contemporary linguistics in this guide (not because they're bad, but because they're likely to be unfamiliar to my readers), but this one is worth knowing.

See also PRONOUN and SUBSTANTIVE.

NOVEL.

Many people use the word *novel* to refer to any book—a sloppy habit you should break. A full, proper definition of the word won't be easy; literary critics wrangle over whether many books deserve to be called novels. But virtually every definition of the term includes these four elements:

A novel is *long* (it's not a short story);

A novel is *fictional* (most of the events didn't happen, or at least didn't happen in the way they're described);

A novel is in *prose* (epic poems don't count); and

A novel is a *narrative* (the writer describes a series of events happening over time).

There are inevitably problematic cases. How long is "long"? What about the so-called "nonfiction novels" that became popular in the 1960s (like Truman Capote's *In Cold Blood* or Tom Wolfe's *Electric Kool-Aid Acid Test*)? What about "verse novels" (like Aleksandr Pushkin's *Yevgeny Onegin*)? Some authors mix elements of the novel with other genres; they may include nonfictional elements in their fiction or fictional elements in their nonfiction. All of these borderline cases can be grounds for legitimate argument.

But don't use the word willy-nilly for any old book. Chaucer's *Canterbury Tales*, for instance, is not a novel (it's a collection of verse narratives); *Hamlet* is not a novel (it's longish and fictional, but it's a play, not a narrative); *A Narrative of the Life of Frederick Douglass* is not a novel (it's a long prose narrative, but it's nonfiction). Plays, biographies, travel narratives, works of criticism, and so on are not novels.

The same goes for the word *story*: although the term is broader than *novel*, it still applies only to narratives.

NUMBER.

Number—not NUMBERS, for which see below—is a term in GRAMMAR. In English, nouns and verbs can take the *singular* number (for one thing) or the *plural* number (for more than one). Some languages have other possibilities: Homeric Greek, biblical Hebrew, and modern standard Arabic, for instance, have a *dual* number for things that come in pairs; I'm told there are languages with a *trial* number for three things, and some with a *paucal* number for "a few" things.

But modern English has just the two, singular and plural. We mark the PLURALS of most NOUNS with an *s* or *es*. The plurals of most PRONOUNS take different forms: not *I* (first-person singular) but *we* (first-person plural); not *he*, *she*, or *it* (third-person singular) but *they* (third-person plural). Modern standard English doesn't distinguish singular and plural *you*, though forms like *y'all*, *youse*, and *yuns* show that many speakers would like them.

In VERBS, at least most regular verbs, the plural tends to be the "UNINFLECTED" form, and we usually add *s* or *es* to the third-person singular: from the INFINITIVE *to look* we get the third-person singular "he, she, it *looks*."

But you know all this, or at least you do if you've been speaking English for more than a few months. Why should you care? There are a few occasions where even native speakers get tripped up; three come to mind:

One is noun-verb AGREEMENT: a singular subject needs a singular verb; a plural subject needs a plural verb. That's usually obvious, but sometimes gets confusing, especially when you have long and complicated noun phrases: in "one of my neighbors," the subject is *one* and the verb should be singular; in "each of the hundreds of people who've worked with me for the last ten years," the subject is EACH and the verb should be singular.

Another danger spot is the indefinite third person, when you want to refer to a single being but don't want to specify sex: "Like a painter mixing *his/her/their/one's* colors," for instance. It's very common to substitute the third-person plural (*they, their, them*) in such contexts, but it's often frowned on in FORMAL WRITING.

Finally, there are some irregular plurals—DATA, MEDIA, PHENOMENA—that many people assume are singular, but old-timers prefer to pair with plural verb forms. Whether you choose to side with the old-timers or the young hipsters is up to you.

NUMBERS.

Many people are confused about how to work numbers into text. Most guides recommend that you spell out small numbers, with "small" meaning up to ten, up to twelve, or up to a hundred (a matter of HOUSE STYLE), and using digits for large numbers. (Newspapers typically use digits more than book publishers do.)

Some other advice: try not to begin a sentence with a numeral: either spell out the number, or RECAST the sentence to move the number from the beginning.

Spell out very large round numbers: not *1,000,000,000*, but *one billion* (an American billion, that is; the British used to use billion for a million million, though they're increasingly using the American standard). If ever you need real precision in expressing large numbers, scientific notation might make sense (see SCIENTIFIC WRITING), but only if you can count on your readers to understand it.

Spell out numbers used to represent orders of magnitude: it's *hundreds of choices*, not *100s of choices*; *thousands of people*, not *1000s of people*.

In a series of numbers, either spell them out or use numerals for *every* member of the list: don't switch in the middle, as in "thirty-two, ninety-six, 107, and 235."

Dates always get numerals: "October 3, 1990" (though there are several competing formats; see DATES).

There's almost never any reason to use both numerals and words for the same number: unless a law firm is paying you enough money to butcher the language with impunity, steer clear of abominations like "two (2)" or "12 (twelve)" (but see LEGAL WRITING).

The only time you should mix spelling and numerals is in very large numbers: not *8,600,000*, but *8.6 million*.

Use numerals for anything difficult to spell out: not *four and sixteen seventeenths*, *thirteen thousand three hundred twenty six*, or *three point one four one five nine*. You can spell out simple fractions like *one-half* or *two-thirds* (the hyphen can come or go, depending on house style).

In large numbers, Americans usually put a comma after every third digit, counting from the right: not 34873274 but 34,873,274. Some guides recommend starting with the comma at 1,000; others write 1000 and 2000 and begin using the comma at 10,000: it's another matter of HOUSE STYLE. Note, though, that you never put commas in some kinds of numbers: years, ZIP codes, page numbers, phone numbers, serial numbers (unless they're in the original). You also don't put them after the decimal point: 1,376.4692.

Obfuscation.

Don't use LONG WORDS where short ones will do; it makes your writing dense and difficult to understand. Words ending in *-ality, -ation, -ize, -ization, -ational,* and so forth are often guilty of making sentences more complex than they need to be. Ask yourself if these suffixes can be removed without damaging the sense: if you can use a shorter form, you probably should; if you can take a big scary noun and make it a punchy and powerful VERB, you probably should. For instance, "The chairman brought about the organization of the conference" can stand to trade that "brought about the organization of" for "organized"—"The chairman organized the conference." Much better.

Many of the entries in this guide—changing METHODOLOGY to *method*, USAGE to *use*, FUNCTIONALITY to *function*—are applications of this tip. See CONCRETE LANGUAGE, LONG WORDS, and VOCABULARY.

Objects.

See DIRECT AND INDIRECT OBJECTS.

Obviously.

See CLEARLY, OBVIOUSLY, UNDOUBTEDLY.

Offensive Language.

See CONNOTATION *VERSUS* DENOTATION, DICTION, EUPHEMISM, and POLITICALLY LOADED LANGUAGE.

Officious.

Officious means not "obliging" or "dutiful" but "meddling" or "impertinent." It's one of those words that sounds positive but actually has a negative meaning, like ENORMITY and FULSOME.

OLD ENGLISH.

Old English, or *Anglo-Saxon*, is the technical term for the language spoken in England from around 500 to around 1100. (The most famous work written in Old English is *Beowulf*; you'll need at least a semester of university-level language study to decode it.) Old English (or OE, as it's often abbreviated) was succeeded by Middle English (ME), the language of Chaucer; and ME was succeeded by Modern English (ModE) around 1500. This means Shakespeare wrote in *modern* English, even though it's loaded with *thee*'s and *doth*'s. You'll keep English teachers happy if you reserve the term *Old English* for truly Old English. See LATINATE *VERSUS* GERMANIC DICTION.

ON A —— BASIS.

Often an unnecessarily long way of saying something. "On a daily basis," for instance, could just as easily be "daily," which can be both an ADJECTIVE and an adverb. (You could also use "every day," but see EVERY DAY *VERSUS* EVERYDAY for an important caveat.) Instead of "The magazine is published on a monthly basis," use "The magazine is published monthly" or "once a month." See ECONOMY.

ON BEHALF OF.

See BEHALF.

ONE.

See SEXIST LANGUAGE AND THE INDEFINITE THIRD PERSON.

ON-LINE *VERSUS* ONLINE.

HOUSE STYLES vary over whether to include the hyphen, though it seems the hyphenless version is winning out. See also E-MAIL and WEB-SITE.

ONLY.

English is a mighty flexible language, and the word *only* can go many places in a sentence. Still, when you're writing and you can't rely on tone of voice to make your meaning clear, it's wise to strive for PRECISION by putting the modifier right before the word or phrase it modifies. "We'll *only write* three papers this semester" might suggest we won't do anything else. "We'll write *only three papers* this semester" makes the meaning clearer. But if it makes your sentence clumsy or UNIDIOMATIC, nix it.

One other thought. The word *only* can mean "solely," "exclusively," or "strictly," but it can also carry CONNOTATIONS of "merely," and a sentence spoken in all innocence can come across sounding dismissive or condescending. If you say someone is "only a waitress," you might want to suggest she doesn't have any other job; others, though, might hear it as a put-down. Be conscious of that, and find another way to express yourself if you fear your audience may be insulted.

Examples:

Weak: I'm only going to say this one time.
We only have one chance to get it right.

Strong: I'm going to say this only one time.
We have only one chance to get it right.

OPUS.

Opus comes from a Latin noun, but don't assume that every Latin noun ending in *-us* gets a PLURAL in *-i*. The proper plural form, both in Latin and in English, is not *opi* but *opera* (yes, it's the origin of our word *opera*). See also CORPUS, GENIUS, GENUS, and VIRUS.

ORIENT *VERSUS* ORIENTATE.

Orientate is the more familiar form in British English, but in Yankeeland you can save a syllable with plain old *orient*.

ORIENTAL.

See POLITICALLY LOADED LANGUAGE.

OXFORD COMMA.

See COMMAS.

PARAGRAPHS.

There's no hard-and-fast rule for the length of a paragraph: it can be as short as a sentence or as long as it has to be. Just remember that each paragraph should contain only one developed idea. A paragraph often begins with a *topic sentence* which sets the tone of the paragraph; the rest amplifies, clarifies, or explores the topic sentence. When you change topics, start a new paragraph.

Be sure your paragraphs are organized to help your argument along. Each paragraph should build on what came before, and should lay the groundwork for whatever comes next. Mastering TRANSITIONS can make a big difference in your writing.

A matter of MECHANICS and HOUSE STYLE: it's customary (at least in America) to indicate new paragraphs in most prose by INDENTING the first line (three to five spaces), with no skipped lines between paragraphs. Business memos and press releases tend to skip a line and not indent. In papers for English classes, don't-skip-but-indent is preferable.

PARAMETER.

A nasty word, forgivable only if you're a mathematician, a scientist, or a computer programmer. (Even then, I'll forgive you only grudgingly.) The rest of the world can safely do without.

PARAPHRASE.

To paraphrase is to take someone else's meaning and to put it into your own words. Note that not only the words but the syntax have to be your own. It's not enough to take someone else's sentence and to go through it substituting SYNONYMS: if you're asked to paraphrase something, the structure of the sentences should be your own, too. Simply replacing every third word doesn't save you from charges of plagiarism.

See also the Citation section at the end of this guide.

Parentheses.

Don't bury important ideas in parentheses. Prof. Daniel White of the University of Toronto gives an example that points out the danger of using parentheses for important thoughts:

> The American and French Revolutions (which provided the inspiration for Blake's prophetic poetry) were very important to English writers of the 1780s and '90s.

Here the substantial part of the sentence is buried in a parenthesis, while the weaker part (note the word "IMPORTANT") is in the main clause. See also EMPHASIS.

Remember that sentence-ending periods should go *outside* the parentheses if the parenthetical remark is part of a larger sentence, but *inside* the parentheses if it's not embedded in a larger sentence. This is an example of the first (notice the punctuation goes outside, because we're still part of that outer sentence). (This is an example of the second, because we're no longer inside any other sentence; the parenthesis is its own sentence.)

Participles.

See DANGLING PARTICIPLES.

Particular.

This particular word, in many particular circumstances, usually serves no particular purpose. Give particular attention to the particular prospect of cutting it out.

Parts of Speech.

Old-fashioned grammars stated that there were eight parts of speech:

> VERBS, which show *action* or states of *being*: *go, talk, eradicate, be, exist,* and so on.

Nouns, which can be *people*, *places*, or *things*: *Napoleon*, *Pittsburgh*, *table*, *eagerness*.

Pronouns, which "stand in for" a noun: *he*, *she*, *it*, *they*, *that*.

Adjectives, which modify a noun or pronoun: *big*, *sleepy*, *stupid*, *dilatory*.

Adverbs, which modify verbs, adjectives, or other adverbs: *easily*, *obviously*, *very*.

Prepositions, which indicate the relationship between various elements in a sentence: *to*, *with*, *from*.

Conjunctions, which link (*conjoin*) parts of a sentence: *and*, *but*, *or*, *because*, *if*, *although*.

Interjections, which are words that don't fit into any of the categories: *hey*, *ouch*, *yo*, *cheers*, *damn*.

All of that's worth knowing and understanding, but don't treat that number eight as an article of faith. Here are a few lessons about this messy language we speak.

First, although dictionaries usually tell you the part of speech for each word, it's not that simple. In many languages, parts of speech are clearly marked in the form of each word: Latin *umbra*, for instance, can only be a noun ("shade"). If you want the verb, it's *umbro*; if you want an adjective, it's *umbrosus*. In English, though, we don't clearly signal parts of speech in our word forms, and words have a habit of being used in various ways: think of *in the shade* (*shade* as a noun), *a shade tree* (as an adjective), and *shade your eyes* (as a verb). Nouns can function as adjectives: *department*, for example, is a noun; but put it in front of another noun—*department store*—and now it functions as an adjective, modifying the word *store*. (The two-word noun phrase *department store* can in turn become an adjective if we put it in front of another noun—"I don't want to pay *department store prices*"—and the three-word noun phrase can in turn become another adjective, and so on, for as long as your ingenuity holds up.) Adjectives can also function as nouns in a sentence: "Sleep is for *the weak*." Here *weak*—which we usually think of as an adjective—is operating "absolutely," and it's playing the role of a noun. Take the adjective *dark* and stick it in front of an adjective like *green*, and now it's acting as an adverb.

Rather than thinking of parts of speech as properties of specific words, then, it's better to think of them as *functions* within a sentence. These functions can be played by single words or groups of words.

Second, English is a very flexible language—it always has been; this isn't some horrible modern development—and words have a habit of changing their parts of speech over time. Some are now perfectly acceptable: although *move* began its life as a verb (with the associated nouns *movement* and *motion*), no one objects to its use as a noun today ("She showed me some impressive moves"; "He took his opponent's rook on his fourth move"; "This is our third move this year"). *Block* went the other way, from a noun to a verb. Other words are still more or less controversial. *LIKE* (as in "this is like that," not "cats like tuna") is traditionally a PREPOSITION, though it's increasingly being used as a CONJUNCTION, and most likely that will someday be the norm; *to transition*, though common in businessese, makes some people woozy (it was first used in 1975). And some of these changing parts of speech are clearly NEOLOGISMS or nonce words; while they probably won't become part of STANDARD ENGLISH, they don't present any serious trouble: "We had to *bookcase-over* the hole in the wall so the landlord wouldn't see it." That one is unlikely to catch on, but some do. You might not like it—as Bill Watterson put it in a brilliant *Calvin and Hobbes* strip, "Verbing weirds language"—and many of them are UGLY, but that's the way the language works.

Finally, don't get too hung up on exactly which part of speech a word is playing, and don't approach the "eight parts of speech" with fundamentalist rigor. We use these terms to describe the language; to force the language into the categories is to put the cart before the etc. A good, modern, technical grammar will give you some more insight into how the language really works.

Passive Voice.

The active VOICE takes the form of "A *does* B"; the passive takes the form of "B *is done* [by A]."

Writers are often told to avoid the passive voice, and there are two reasons for this advice. The first is that sentences often become dense and clumsy when they're filled with passive constructions. The more serious danger of the passive voice, though, is that it lets the writer shirk the responsibility of providing a subject for the verb—the agent disappears altogether. Daniel White of the University of Toronto gives an example:

> "I'm sorry that the paper was poorly written." If you're going to apologize, apologize: "I'm sorry I wrote a bad paper." The active voice forces one to be specific and confident, not wimpy.

The stakes only get higher when you talk about atrocities worse than bad papers. This is why nefarious government and corporate spokesmen are so fond of the passive voice: think of the notorious all-purpose excuse, "Mistakes were made." Then think about how much weaseling is going on in a sentence like "It has been found regrettable that the villagers' lives were terminated"—notice how the agency has disappeared altogether. It should make you shudder.

In your own writing, therefore, favor the active voice whenever you can. Instead of the passive "The point will *be made*," try the active "I will *make* the point"—notice the agent ("I") is still there.

Don't go overboard, though. Some passives are necessary and useful. In SCIENTIFIC WRITING, for instance, sentences are routinely written in the passive voice; the authors are therefore given less importance, and the facts are made to speak for themselves. Even in non-scientific writing, you can't (and shouldn't) avoid all passives.

Don't confuse *am, is, are, to be*, and such with the passive voice, and don't confuse ACTION VERBS with the *active voice*.

The real question is whether the subject of the sentence is *doing* anything, or having something *done to* it. *I have been carrying* is active, while *I have been carried* is passive.

PER.

Avoid the businessese habit of using *per* instead of *according to*, as in *per manufacturers' guidelines.* Ick.

PERIODS.

This isn't a comprehensive guide to period usage; that would take more space than I can spare. Besides, you already know most of the rules: a period ends a declarative sentence, and sometimes is used in abbreviations. Still, a few things aren't obvious.

For instance: when *do* you use periods in ACRONYMS or other abbreviations? Alas, there's no reliable rule: some get periods, some don't, and only a DICTIONARY will tell you for sure which they are. (Even the dictionaries are only reporting on their sense of the prevailing usage; no one standard is "right," and dictionaries will differ from one another.) A few rough guidelines, though, may help. Academic degrees usually get periods (Ph.D., D.Ed.), as do awards and other distinctions (F.R.S. for Fellow of the Royal Society, D.S.C. for Distinguished Service Cross). Abbreviations usually presented in lowercase (e.g., i.e., a.m., etc.) usually get periods. ACRONYMS—abbreviations that form pronounceable words (NASA, AIDS, NIMBY)—usually go without.

But these are only rough guidelines, not hard-and-fast rules. Different HOUSE STYLES treat words in different ways; they leave a lot uncovered altogether; and they don't address those wacky abbreviations that take other forms (like A/C for air conditioning). Hie thee to the dictionary and, if you're writing for publication, don't be surprised if your editor overrules you.

More important: what if one of those abbreviations with a period appears at the end of a sentence?—do you use another period to end the sentence, or is one enough?

This one is simple enough: never double up periods. If a sentence ends with "etc." the period in the abbreviation does double duty, serving as the full stop to end the sentence. If, however, you need another mark of punctuation after an abbreviation, you can put it after the period. So:

> This was her first trip to the U.S. (The period does double-duty, ending both the abbreviation and the sentence.)

> Is this your first trip to the U.S.? (The period ends the abbreviation, but the question mark ends the sentence.)

> On her first trip to the U.S., Kristina lost her passport. (The period ends the abbreviation, but the sentence keeps going after the comma.)

The only thing to remember: don't double the periods. Everything else is logical enough.

See also ELLIPSES.

PERSON.

Grammarians have divided references to people into three categories, to refer to *I*, *you*, and *he or she*. The *first person* is I, me, my, we, our, and so on. The *second person* is you and your. The *third person* is he, she, they, their, his, hers, him, her, and so on. While you need to pay close attention to these when you study a foreign language, most issues of person are instinctive to native English speakers. For the few times when you should pay attention, see SHALL *VERSUS* WILL and SEXIST LANGUAGE AND THE INDEFINITE THIRD PERSON.

On a related topic, some people have been taught *never* to use the first person in their writing. There's something to this: your attention should be on the work you're discussing, not on yourself (unless, of course, the assignment specifically calls for a personal essay). Your reader has little reason to care about you. And there's no need for endless qualifications: "I think," "I believe," "it seems to me," that sort of thing. Readers will take it for granted that the paper represents your thoughts and beliefs, so there's no need to draw attention to that fact.

Still, many people take this principle too far, and resort to the Victorian pomposity of the first-person plural ("We have argued in the previous paragraph") or bizarre contortions to turn first-person references into third-person ("The writer of this essay") when a simple "I" or "me" would be much more direct and forceful. Don't bend over backwards to avoid using the first person: there are many times when it's the best choice.

PERSONALIZED.

Personalized means *made personal*, and suggests that something was not personal but now is. This isn't what you mean in phrases like *personalized attention*. Use *personal*. See OBFUSCATION.

PERUSE.

A tricky one. The traditional meaning of *peruse* is (in the words of the *OED*) "To examine in detail; to scrutinize, inspect, survey, oversee; to consider, to take heed of," or (in the words of the *American Heritage Dictionary*) "To read or examine, typically with great care." The *per-* prefix here means "thoroughly, completely, to completion, to the end." But *peruse* is increasingly being used to mean "to look over briefly or superficially; to browse" (*OED*) or "to glance over, skim" (*AHD*).

Most PRESCRIPTIVE guides will tell you the "skim" meaning is simply wrong: Bryan Garner writes (in *A Dictionary of Modern American Usage*) that "Some writers misuse the word as if it meant 'to read quickly' or 'scan,'" and two out of three members of the *American Heritage* Usage Panel find this meaning unacceptable. On the other hand, my guess is that only a tiny fraction of the reading public knows the "real" meaning, so you can't count on them to understand you if you use it. Advise people to peruse a memo, and they'll probably think it means "glance at it." Your best bet, then, is probably to avoid the word, unless you're certain your readers will get your meaning.

PHENOMENA.

A PLURAL noun: the singular is *phenomenon*. Don't speak of "a phenomena."

PHRASAL VERBS.

The traditional notion of the PARTS OF SPEECH assumes that each VERB is a single word, perhaps paired with a PREPOSITION or adverb. In English, though, many of our most common verbs are actually made up of multiple words. Consider a word like *take*, and all the meanings it takes on as we pair it with other particles: *take up, take off, take on, take to, take over*. Since it's the whole phrase that carries the meaning, and since you can't easily deduce the resulting meaning even if you know the words separately, these *phrasal verbs* usually get their own entries in dictionaries.

PLURALS.

Plural means "more than one." English handles these things more simply than many languages. You already know the basic rules: most NOUNS take an *-s* or *-es* at the end; singular nouns ending in *-y* usually end in *-ies* in the plural. Our ADJECTIVES don't change form at all. There are a handful of irregular nouns—*child, children*; *woman, women*—but native speakers learn the important ones early, and non-native speakers can find a list of them easily enough.

A few exceptions require special care. In some noun phrases, the "head noun" gets the plural, even if it's not at the end of the noun phrase: *mothers in law, attorneys general, courts martial*. Such forms may be disappearing, but they're still preferred in most formal writing.

Some words imported from other languages have irregular plurals: many Latin nouns in *-us*, for instance, take *-i* in the plural (but not all: see VIRUS); many nouns ending in *-um* take a plural in *-a* (*dicta, moratoria*); many nouns ending in *-trix* take a plural in *-trices* (*matrices, dominatrices*). Sometimes foreign words have both a foreign plural and an English plural, both in circulation in English: consider *index*, which can have the Latin plural *indices* or the English plural *indexes*, or *compendium*, which is sometimes pluralized as *compendia* and sometimes as *compendiums*. Sometimes they have different meanings; sometimes they're perfectly interchangeable. Check a DICTIONARY if you have any hesitation, and don't assume everything ending in -*us* gets a plural in -*i*.

Probably because some of these foreign plurals can look singular to English-speakers, many words that began as plurals are increasingly being used as though they were singular. A few former plurals are now solidly in the singular camp: *agenda*, for instance, was originally the plural of *agendum*, and meant "things to be done." Nowadays, though, even the fussiest pedant won't gripe about singular *agenda*, plural *agendas*—the Latin origins are largely forgotten. A few other Latin plurals, though, aren't yet lost causes, and purists prefer to keep treating them as plurals.

Many people get spooked by the plurals of proper names, but the rules aren't that different. Papa Smith, Mama Smith, and Baby Smith are the Smiths; Mr. Birch, Mrs. Birch, and Junior Birch are the Birches. The only difference between proper and common nouns is that proper names ending in -*y* shouldn't change form in the plural: just add an -*s*. The members of the Percy family are the Percys, not the Percies.

Resist the urge to put an APOSTROPHE before the *s* in a plural, whether in common or proper nouns. The term for this vulgar error is the "greengrocer's apostrophe," from the shopkeepers' habit of advertising their "potato's" and "apple's." The only occasions on which you use apostrophes to make plurals are spelled out in my entry for APOSTROPHES.

For a few less-than-obvious plurals, see APPARATUS, CORPUS, DATA, GENIUS, GENUS, MEDIA, OPUS, PHENOMENA, POLITICS, SPECIES, and VIRUS.

Plus.

The use of the word *plus* where *and* or *with* would be better is a bad habit picked up from advertising copy. Try to limit *plus* to mathematics, and use *and* or *with* where they're appropriate.

Politically Loaded Language.

I'll assume my readers don't go out of their way to offend strangers—at least, most of my readers and most of the time. But it's all too easy to give offense without even trying, because a word that you find perfectly neutral may enrage someone else.

A whole class of words—especially those that identify groups of people by race, ethnicity, nationality, religion, gender, sexual preference, bodily or mental health, and so on, but also those that refer to politically contested regions or behaviors—can generate a lot of passion. It'd be swell if we could simply call everyone what they wish to be called, but you can't always conduct surveys to find out, and not everyone in any large population is going to have the same preferences. The world too easily falls into factions, and a term that keeps one side happy may make the other side positively irate. Use a word like *retarded*—to half the world you're an insensitive, reactionary, thick-skinned troglodyte. Use *mentally challenged*—to the other half you're a pandering, spineless, politically correct, mealy-mouthed euphemizer. Ya just can't win.

Now, there may be times when you *want* to declare an allegiance with one side or another, and intentionally use a term that part of your audience will love and the other part will hate. You may even want to needle one side by intentionally choosing a word that will get under their skin. Many Republicans enjoy using *Democrat* rather than *Democratic* as an adjective—"the Democrat party," "Democrat policies"—because they know it irritates Democrats. The left does the same with other terms. In many cases, though, you want to keep readers of many political persuasions on your side. The challenge for a writer, then, is to find a vocabulary that alienates no one, without being so obvious about avoiding offense that you're open to charges of being "politically correct."

(An excursus: the term *politically correct* is itself politically loaded. Few people describe themselves that way; for most of its modern history it has been meant as an insult. Many of the scariest examples of "political correctness run amok"—a phrase Google tells me has been used nearly 38,000 times— were never used by real people, invented by those who wanted to make the whole enterprise seem ridiculous. The euphemism *vertically challenged*, a supposed replacement for *short*, has, as far as I can make out, always been used ironically.)

Sometimes the terms divide neatly into three categories—one set for proponents of an issue, another set for those on the opposite side, but also a term or two in the middle with no strong connotations that can be used without danger. Often, though, there's no value-neutral term, and you have to cast your lot with one camp or another. It's close to impossible to talk about the Middle East without offending some portion of your readership, based on whether you refer to, say, *Palestine*, the *Palestinian territories*, the *occupied territories*, the *disputed territories*, and so on. Political groups maneuver to force you to make a choice between charged terms. For those who favor access to legal abortion, the divide is between *pro-choice* and *anti-choice* (or even *anti-woman*); for those who would restrict access to legal abortion, the divide is between *pro-life* and *anti-life* (or *pro-abortion* or even *pro-death*). Depending on what you think of their cause, the same group of people might be *terrorists*, *rebels*, *insurgents*, or *freedom-fighters*. Another group might be *illegals* or *undocumented immigrants*. There are squabbles over whether adults without children are *childless* (implying some kind of deprivation) or *child-free* (implying a choice). Some find *pet* degrading, and prefer *animal companion*.

This state of things leaves me in a bind. It's not for me to determine your political beliefs, and I'll have no truck with censorship. I don't want to advocate spineless acquiescence to every pressure group with a beef about a word, and I don't want to encourage the thoughtless use of terms that offend innocents. But if you're going to keep your audience on your side, you have to choose your words carefully, especially when you venture into this kind of politically charged language.

There's no room here for a comprehensive list of risky words. Many things you should avoid are obvious—the notorious "N-word" has now passed even the "F-word" as the most offensive in the language, and I won't bother listing things that you already know. I can, however, list a few trouble spots that may be less than self-evident. In your own writing, make whatever use of this advice you think appropriate.

> Be careful with terms that seem to lump everyone who shares some trait together into one uniform group. Saying things about "gays" or "Hispanics," as if all gay people or all Hispanic people think alike, can easily give offense. A phrase like "you people," even if spoken innocently, can strike some people as terribly demeaning.

> Although *homosexual* was for a long time a value-neutral term, its appropriation by the cultural right has made it offensive, or at least a little irritating, to many gay people. Unfortunately that leaves you with the need to recite a long catalogue of sexual identities if you want to be maximally inclusive: "lesbian, gay, bisexual, and transgendered," for instance. (There's not the same trouble with the general noun *homosexuality*.)

> Remember that some terms have broader application than might be obvious on first thought. In America, the word *Asian*—now much more widely favored than *Oriental*—usually applies to East Asia (China, Japan, Korea, Mongolia) and sometimes to Southeast Asia (including Vietnam, Cambodia, and Thailand). But remember that it also includes South Asia (including India, Pakistan, Bangladesh, Sri Lanka, and Nepal), Central Asia (including Kazakhstan, Turkmenistan, and Uzbekistan), and so on.

> Avoid the word *ethnic* to refer to anyone other than white Anglos—it can imply that whites aren't an ethnicity.

We usually have no trouble identifying nationalities, ethnicities, and religions with the definite ARTICLE and an adjective: the French, the Chinese, the Catholics. But because of a long and very unpleasant history, the phrases "the Jews" and "the blacks" often give offense. Don't let it paralyze you, and don't contort yourself into strange shapes to avoid the phrases when they're the obvious ones to use, but do be conscious of the possibility for offense.

Sometimes a group has co-opted a term that was once used disparagingly and begun to use it proudly. One of the more famous examples is *queer*, once used as an offensive taunt aimed particularly at gay men, but now often used by many gay activists. In cases like this you have to be careful; a word used by some group may be offensive if it's spoken by an outsider.

Sometimes older terms, no longer in favor, survive in the names of organizations and publications: the NAACP, for instance, is the National Association for the Advancement of Colored People, but virtually none of their members would use a term like "colored" today; the American Moslem Foundation now uses the spelling *Muslim* in all their literature, but the older *Moslem* persists in the name of the group. In these cases, use their proper names, but don't assume that automatically licenses you to use the touchy words in other contexts.

I wish I had good advice for every situation, but one size refuses to fit all. Besides, if I were to recommend specific terms, the list would become obsolete pretty quickly; what was polite in Grandma's day might be grotesquely offensive today. Only one piece of advice is always relevant: think of the effect your language will have on your AUDIENCE (but you should know that by now).

See also A.D., AFRICAN AMERICAN, BRITAIN, COMMUNITY, EUPHEMISM, MAN, MOSLEM *VERSUS* MUSLIM, Ms, and NORMAL, SHIBBOLETHS.

POLITICS.

The *s* and the end can be confusing: is *politics* singular or PLURAL?

If you're referring to the subject of politics, it's singular: "Politics is an obsession inside the Beltway," for example, or "Politics is the art of the possible." But when you're referring to one person's, party's, or nation's collection of beliefs and practices, it's usually treated as a plural: "Her politics are deeply offensive"; "The politics of the French are often confusing."

The story is similar for a number of nouns ending in *-ics*: *acoustics, economics, ethics, mathematics, physics,* and so on.

POLYSYNDETON.

See ASYNDETON AND POLYSYNDETON.

POSSESSIVE.

The *possessive* is used to indicate *belonging*: *Carol's car* ("the car that belongs to Carol"), *my brother's apartment* ("the apartment that belongs to my brother"), *my neighbors' yard* ("the yard that belongs to my neighbors"), *his name* ("the name that belongs to him"), and so on. You could also express most of them with *of*: "the car of Carol," "the apartment of my brother," "the yard of my neighbors," "the name of him."

The rules for forming possessives are simple:

> The personal PRONOUNS have their own possessive forms: *my* ("belonging to me"), *your* ("belonging to you"), *his* ("belonging to him"), *her* ("belonging to her"), *our* ("belonging to us"), and *their* ("belonging to them").

> With most singular nouns, you form the possessive with an APOSTROPHE and *s*: *Carol's, brother's*.

> With plural nouns ending in *s*, just add an apostrophe: *neighbors'*. Personal names don't get treated any differently:

Bush's agenda ("the agenda that belongs to Bush"), *the Smiths' house* ("the house that belongs to the Smiths").

Plural nouns that don't end in *s* are treated like singular nouns, with apostrophe and *s*: *the people's choice, the children's toys*, and so on.

The only time for hesitation is when you have a singular noun that ends in *-s* or an *s* sound: *bus, James, house*. This is a matter of HOUSE STYLE: most guides suggest the same rules as before: *the bus's route, James's friends, my house's roof*. Others (especially in journalism) suggest just an apostrophe without the additional *s*. Some have different rules depending on whether the *s* is sounded like an *s* or a *z*; some have different rules based on whether it's a word of one syllable or more. But it's usually best to go with apostrophe-*s* with all singular nouns, whether or not they end in *s*.

PRECISION.

The guiding principle in all your word choices should be precision, the most important contributor to CLARITY.

Sometimes this means choosing words a little out of the ordinary: *peripatetic* might come closer to the mark than *wandering*, and *recondite* is sometimes more accurate than *obscure*. But while a large VOCABULARY will help you here, don't resort to LONG WORDS or OBFUSCATION; it does you no good to pick the perfect word if your readers don't know it. More often precision means choosing the right familiar word: paying attention to easily CONFUSED PAIRS like IMPLY AND INFER, and making sure the words you choose have exactly the right meaning. For instance, "Hamlet's situation is extremely important in the play" means almost nothing. Try something that expresses a particular idea, like "Hamlet's indecision forces the catastrophe" or "The murder of Hamlet's father brings about the crisis."

Precision can also mean putting your words in just the right order, or using just the right grammatical construction to make your point. Always read your writing as closely as possible, paying attention to every word, and ask yourself whether every word says *exactly* what you mean.

PREDICATE.

A declarative sentence (or independent clause) is made up of two bits, the *subject* and the *predicate*. The subject—usually containing one or more NOUNS or PRONOUNS, along with their accompanying MODIFIERS—is who or what does the action of the sentence. The predicate is what's said about the subject: it consists of the main VERB, along with all its modifiers and objects.

(That simplifies things quite a bit. The subject doesn't have to be a noun or a pronoun; it can be a *that* clause, for instance: "That William Shakespeare wrote the plays attributed to him is beyond doubt." The subject isn't "William Shakespeare," but the whole *that* clause. And some sentences have only "dummy" noun phrases, like "It's raining," where the *it* means nothing.)

Why should you care? In some style guides, some COMPOUND modifiers—especially when ADVERBS that don't end in *-ly* modify adjectives—are HYPHENATED when they appear in the "attributive" position, but not in the "predicate" position. In other words, there's no hyphen if the adjective phrase is what is being predicated. That *usually* means they should be hyphenated when they come before the noun they modify, but not after, although that's not always the case. For example:

Shakespeare's *least-read* play is probably *Two Gentlemen of Verona*. (The phrase is hyphenated because it's attributive.)

Of all of Shakespeare's plays, *Two Gentlemen of Verona* is probably the *least read*. (No hyphen because it's in the predicate position.)

He gives a series of *well-chosen* examples. (Attributive, and therefore hyphenated.)

His examples are always *well chosen*. (No hyphen.)

It's a subtle distinction, and not one to get too worked up about. Some style guides are backing away from this rule, preferring to give the general advice that such phrases should be hyphenated whenever they aid clarity.

PREPOSITIONS.

Prepositions are usually little words that indicate direction, position, location, and so forth. Some examples: *to, with, from, at, in, near, by, beside,* and *above.*

A quick-and-dirty rule of thumb: you can usually recognize a preposition by putting it before the word *he.* If your ear tells you *he* should be *him,* the word might be a preposition. Thus *to* plus *he* becomes *to him,* so *to* is a preposition. (This doesn't help with verbs of action; *show + he* becomes *show him.* Still, it might help in some doubtful cases.)

PREPOSITIONS AT THE END.

Along with SPLIT INFINITIVES, a favorite BUGBEAR of the traditionalists. Whatever the merit of the RULE—and both historically and logically, there's not much—there's a substantial body of opinion against end-of-sentence prepositions; if you want to keep the sticklers happy, try to avoid ending written sentences (and clauses) with prepositions, such as *to, with, from, at,* and *in,* especially in FORMAL WRITING. Instead of "The topics we want to write on," where the preposition *on* ends the clause, consider "The topics on which we want to write." Prepositions should usually go before (*pre-position*) the words they govern.

On the other hand—and it's a big other hand—the sticklers shouldn't always dictate your writing, and you don't deserve your writing license if you elevate this rough guideline into a superstition. Don't let it make your writing clumsy or obscure; if a sentence is more GRACEFUL with a final preposition, let it stand. For instance, "He gave the public what it longed for" is clear and idiomatic, even though it ends with a preposition; "He gave the public that for which it longed" avoids the problem but doesn't look like English. "There's nothing to worry about" is dandy even in formal settings, whereas "There's nothing about which to worry" would provoke confused stares.

A sentence becomes unnecessarily obscure when it's filled with *from whom*s and *with which*es. According to a widely circulated (and often mutated) story, Winston Churchill, reprimanded for ending a sentence with a preposition, put it best: "This is the sort of English up with which I will not put."

Examples:

Disputed: Who did you give it to?
Which page did you find it on?

Preferred: To whom did you give it?
On which page did you find it?

PRESCRIPTIVE *VERSUS* DESCRIPTIVE GRAMMARS.

The grammar books you're used to are what linguists call *prescriptive*: that is, they *prescribe* RULES for proper usage. For several hundred years, "grammar" was synonymous with "prescriptive grammar." You went to a book to get the definitive ruling: thou shalt not SPLIT INFINITIVES, thou shalt not end sentences with PREPOSITIONS. (This is presumably why you're reading this guide now: to find out what's "right" and what's "wrong.")

Professional linguists today are justly suspicious about such things, and most spend their time on *descriptive* grammars: descriptions of how people *really* speak and write, instead of rules on how they *should*. They're doing important work, not least by arguing that no language or dialect is *inherently* better than any other. They've done a signal service in reminding us that Black English is as "legitimate" a dialect as the Queen's English, and that speaking the way Jane Austen writes doesn't make you more righteous than someone who uses *y'all*. They've also demonstrated that many self-styled "grammar" experts know next to nothing about GRAMMAR as it's studied by professionals, and many aren't much better informed about the history of the language. Many prescriptive guides are grievously ill informed.

Fair enough. Sometimes, though, I enjoy picking fights with those linguists, usually amateur, who try to crowd prescription out of the market altogether. The dumber ones make a leap from "No language is inherently better than another" (which is true) to "Everything's up for grabs" (which is baloney). The worst are hypocrites who, after attacking the very idea of rules, go on to prescribe their own, usually the opposite of whatever the traditionalists say. These folks have allowed statistics to take the place of judgment, relying on the principle, "Whatever most people say is the best."

These dullards forget that words are used in social situations, and that even if something isn't *inherently* good or evil, it might still have a good or bad effect on your audience. I happen to know for a fact that God doesn't care whether you split infinitives. But some people do, and that's a simple fact that no statistical table will change. A good descriptivist should tell you that. My beef with many descriptivists is that they don't describe *enough*. A really thorough description of a word or usage would take into account not only how many people use it, but in what circumstances and to what effect.

Much can be said against old-fashioned BUGBEARS like end-of-sentence prepositions and singular *they*. They're not particularly logical, they don't have much historical justification, and they're difficult even for native speakers to learn. But you don't always get to choose your audience, and some of your readers or hearers will think less of you if you break the "rules." Chalk it up to snobbishness if you like, but it's a fact. To pick an even more politically charged example, Black English is a rich and fascinating dialect with its own sophisticated lexicon and syntax. But using it in certain social situations just hurts the speaker's chances of getting what he or she wants. That's another brute fact—one with the worst of historical reasons, but a fact still, and wishing it away won't change it.

That doesn't mean the old-fashioned prescriptivists should always be followed slavishly: it means you have to exercise *judgment* in deciding which rules to apply when. Here's the principle that guides what I write and say whenever traditional ("correct") usage differs from colloquial ("incorrect") usage.

Does the traditional usage, hallowed by prescriptive grammars and style guides, improve the CLARITY or PRECISION of the sentence? If so, use the traditional usage.

Does the colloquial usage add clarity or precision to the more traditional version?—if so, use the colloquial one, rules be damned.

Sometimes the traditional usage, the one you've been taught is "right," is downright clumsy or UNIDIOMATIC. The classic example is "It's I," which, though "right"—traditionalists will tell you *it* is in the nominative case, and that a copulative verb requires the same case in the subject and the predicate—is too stilted for all but the most formal situations. "It's me" sounds a thousand times more natural. If you like being the sort of person who says "It's I," that's fine, but know that most of your audience, including most of the educated part of your audience, will find it out of place.

If neither one is *inherently* better, for reasons of logic, clarity, or whatever, is the traditional form intrusive? If it's not going to draw attention to itself, I prefer to stick with the "correct" usage, even if the reasons for its being "correct" are dubious. For instance, the word ONLY can go many places in a sentence. Putting it in a position the sticklers call "wrong" will probably distract a few readers; putting it in a position the traditionalists call "right" won't bother anyone, even those who are less hung up about word placement. In this case, unlike the "It's I" case, following the "rule" will keep the traditionalists happy without irritating the rest of the world.

For me it's a simple calculation: which usage, the traditional or the colloquial, is going to be more effective? Since *most* traditional usages work in *most* colloquial settings, and since *many* colloquial usages don't work in FORMAL settings, I usually opt for the traditional usage.

(A parenthesis: no matter how conscientiously you try, you'll never keep *everyone* in your reading audience happy. People have all sorts of wacky hangups, and everything you could conceivably say is bound to alienate someone. You can, however, avoid the things that are known to make large numbers of people unhappy.)

Some determined iconoclasts consider it pandering to follow any traditional rule they don't like, and do everything they can to flout the old grammar books. I suppose some think wanton infinitive-splitting shows the world what free spirits they are, and some think giving in to "White English" is unmitigated Uncle-Tomism.

Maybe. If rebellion makes you happy, go nuts; I won't stop you. But as I make clear throughout this guide, writing is for me a matter of having an impact on an audience, and my experience, if it's worth anything, is that some usages help you and some hurt you. Think about each one, not in terms of what you're "allowed" to say, but in terms of what your words can do for you. A dogmatic prejudice against the rules is no better than a dogmatic prejudice in their favor.

See AUDIENCE, GRAMMAR, RULES, and TASTE.

PRESENTLY.

Presently traditionally means "very soon" or "immediately": "She'll arrive presently"; "I'll get to it presently." Avoid using it to mean "now," not least because we've already got a perfectly good word that means "now"—viz., *now*—that's one syllable instead of three. Besides, the present TENSE is usually all you need.

See also CURRENTLY.

PRESIDENT.

See CAPITALIZATION.

PREVIOUS.

Overused. *Earlier* may be more to the point, and *previous* is often redundant, as in "Our *previous* discussion." Unless you mean to distinguish that discussion from another one (such as "the discussion before the one I just mentioned"), leave out *previous*, since you're not likely to mention discussions you haven't had yet.

Principal *versus* Principle.

Principal can be either an ADJECTIVE or a NOUN; *principle* is strictly a noun.

Principal, adjective: chief, main, leading, most important.

Principal, noun: the most important person or group of people ("After much debate, the two *principals* reached an agreement"); the head of a school (the *principal* person in the administration); borrowed money (as distinct from *interest*).

Principle (always a noun): a rule, standard, law, guideline, or doctrine.

Worth keeping straight. The most common booboo is probably using *principle* as an adjective. Don't.

Prior to.

For a less stuffy and bureaucratic tone, replace *prior to* or *prior* with *before* or *earlier* whenever possible.

Pronoun.

A pronoun takes the place of a noun: it *stands for* (Latin *pro-*) a noun. Pronouns include *he*, *it*, *her*, *me*, and so forth. Instead of saying "Bob gave Terry a memo Bob wrote, and Terry read the memo," we'd use the nouns *Bob*, *Terry*, and *memo* only once, and let pronouns do the rest: "Bob gave Terry a memo *he* wrote, and *she* read *it*."

There are a few special sorts of pronouns: POSSESSIVE pronouns, such as *my*, *hers*, and *its*, which mean *of* something or *belonging to* something; and relative pronouns, such as *whose* and *which*, that connect a *relative clause* to a sentence: "She read the memo, *which* mentioned the new system." (For a warning on relative pronouns, see SENTENCE FRAGMENTS.)

PRONUNCIATION.

Lord knows this guide irritates enough people already; I don't want to alienate the rest of the Anglophone world by issuing decrees on how words should be pronounced. My concern in this guide is with the written rather than the spoken language. But many things I've said about writing apply to speech as well. Start with the entry for SHIBBOLETHS, and follow some of the cross-references from there.

If you have any questions about orthoepy—a delightfully obscure word that means "proper pronunciation"—start with a good DICTIONARY. Though it takes a while to get the hang of it, consider learning IPA (the International Phonetic Alphabet), which allows greater precision in rendering pronunciations (it distinguishes the *th* sound in *thin* from the one in *they*, for instance, to say nothing of the two sounds that the letters *th* make in *hothead*). And Charles Harrington Elster has written a few enjoyable books on the subject, collected into one omnibus volume as *The Big Book of Beastly Mispronunciations: The Complete Opinionated Guide for the Careful Speaker* (Boston: Houghton Mifflin, 1999).

PROOFREADING.

You should always read over your wrok carefully before handing it to someone esle, looking for typoos, mispelled words, problems with AGREEMENT, words that missing, and so on. There's nothing wrong with using a SPELLING CHECKER, but they routinely miss so many things that you still have to read your work closely. (Don't depend on GRAMMAR CHECKERS, which usually make your writing worse, not better.)

Remember, though, that proofreading is only one part of the REVISION process.

PUNCTUATION.

See separate entries for various punctuation marks: COLONS, COMMAS, ELLIPSES, EXCLAMATION POINTS, PERIODS,

PUNCTUATION AND QUOTATION MARKS, SEMICOLONS, and
SINGLE QUOTATION MARKS.

PUNCTUATION AND QUOTATION MARKS.

In America, commas and periods go *inside* quotation marks,
while semicolons and colons go *outside*, regardless of the
punctuation in the original quotation. Question marks
and exclamation points depend on whether the question or
exclamation is part of the quotation, or part of the sentence
containing the quotation. Some examples:

> See the chapter called "The Conclusion, in which Nothing
> is Concluded." (Periods always go inside.)
>
> The spokesman called it "shocking," and called
> immediately for a committee. (Commas always go inside.)
>
> Have you read "Araby"? (The question mark is part of the
> outer sentence, not the quoted part, so it goes outside.)
>
> He asked, "How are you?" (The question mark is part of
> the quoted material, so it goes inside.)

Note that in American USAGE, all quoted material goes in
"double quotation marks," except for quotations within
quotations, which get SINGLE QUOTATION MARKS.

There are a very few instances where it's wise to put the
punctuation outside the quotation marks—cases where it's
really important whether the punctuation mark is part of
the quotation or not. A software manual, for instance, might
have to make it very clear whether the period is part of a
command or simply ends the sentence in which the command
appears: getting it wrong means the command won't work.
Bibliographers are concerned with the exact form of the
punctuation in a book. In these cases, it makes sense.

Most of the time, though—when lives don't depend on
whether the comma is or isn't part of the quotation—stick
with the general usage outlined above; it's what publishers
expect.

Punctuation and Spaces.

The traditional rule, and one especially suited to the monospaced FONTS common in typescripts (as opposed to desktop publishing): put one space after a comma or semicolon; put two spaces after a (sentence-ending) period, exclamation point, or question mark. Colons have been known to go either way. For spaces after quotation marks, base your choice on the punctuation inside the quotation. Publishers often (but not always) use standard word spacing between sentences (it's a matter of HOUSE STYLE), and it seems to be gaining ground among typists today, perhaps through the influence of desktop publishing. In any case, it's nothing to fret about.

See also ELLIPSES.

Quality.

Quality may be the most abused and overused word in business English. The word is a noun, and means *a characteristic* or *a degree of excellence*. Avoid using *quality* as an ADJECTIVE, as in *a quality product*—leave that sort of cant to advertising copywriters. Use *well made, good, useful,* something like that. Don't use *quality* as an adverb, as in *a quality-built product*. Perhaps the best advice is: don't use *quality*. We have so many words in the language that are so much better.

Quite.

Quite is almost always a space-waster; it usually softens sentences that shouldn't be softened. See WASTED WORDS.

Quotation Marks.

See PUNCTUATION AND QUOTATION MARKS.

Quotations.

When you quote others, you're expected to quote them *exactly*, right down to the spelling, capitalization, and italicization. If you change anything, you have to signal it to your readers. The most common ways to do this are with [brackets] for INTERPOLATIONS and ELLIPSES (…) for omissions. (Newspapers sometimes uses parentheses instead of brackets—see JOURNALISM—but square brackets pose less risk of confusion.)

If, for example, your source mentions things that are irrelevant to your argument, you can cut them—as long as you note the fact. Suppose your source reads, "That summer, as noted on p. 327, was one of the hottest on record." The bit about p. 327 doesn't matter a whit to *your* readers, so you can omit it, indicating the omission with an ellipsis: "That summer…was one of the hottest on record." If, on the other hand, your source mentions an "it" or a "she" that's explained elsewhere, you may want to supply the missing reference in brackets:

"Prosecutors said [Ms Patel] stabbed her husband in a rage at their modest one-bedroom Baltimore apartment." Or suppose your source has someone speaking in the first person and present tense, but your narrative requires it to be in the third person and past tense, you can make those changes, but you have to indicate them. Suppose your source reads, "I hate to walk through my neighbors' yard." You can adjust it to read "[He] hate[d] to walk through [his] neighbors' yard."

If too many brackets or ellipses threaten to make the passage clumsy, consider rewriting or PARAPHRASING the whole thing. There's usually no need, for instance, to begin or end a quotation with a bracketed interpolation: given the source

> I hate to walk through my neighbors' yard.

you can just move the initial pronoun outside the quotation marks:

> He "hate[d] to walk through [his] neighbors' yard."

Ditto for cases where you omit the beginning or end of a passage: if your source says

> Moreover, as we have already seen, the Spanish language is rich in words derived from Arabic, a Semitic language unrelated to the Indo-European languages

you can trim it without ellipses at the front or back: "the Spanish language is rich in words derived from Arabic." Other minor adjustments like that often make sense.

There are a few exceptions to the general rule about exact quotation, cases where you're allowed to make "silent" changes to your text (that is, without drawing attention to them):

If the original source uses 'SINGLE QUOTATION MARKS' (inverted commas, common in British English), you can silently change them to "double" as appropriate.

If the original source's system of putting punctuation marks inside or outside quotations differs from yours, you can silently adjust the punctuation.

If the original includes footnote references or parenthetical citations, you can silently omit them.

Some HOUSE STYLES allow you to change the capitalization of the first letter in a quotation without indicating it: if, for instance, you begin a sentence with a quotation that comes from the middle of your source's sentence, you can silently change the lowercase to a capital letter. Other style guides say you should use [B]rackets around any letter that changes case.

Obsolete typography—the "long *s*" (the one that looks like an *f*), "running quotation marks" (those that go down the lefthand margin), ligatures like *ct* and *st*—should almost always be changed to reflect modern usage. If you decide to modernize the spelling in any other way, though, you should indicate it somewhere.

What if your source contains a typo?—Are you supposed to fix it, or leave it alone? First, be sure it's really a typo, and not merely an obsolete spelling; some words have changed spelling over the years. If, though, you're sure it's really a typo, you can do one of two things. The first is to quote it exactly as it appears, and then to signal that the typo isn't yours with the word *sic* in brackets—it means "thus" or "this way," and it tells readers "my source really looks like this." (You can tag old spellings this way, too—"If musick [*sic*] be the food of love, play on"—but it's usually not necessary; readers will assume you're following your source. For more details, see SIC.) The other possibility is to make the necessary changes and to put them in brackets. Suppose, for instance, your source is obviously missing a word: "To be or not to be, that the question." You can supply it: "To be or not to be, that [is] the question." Or maybe one letter is obviously wrong: "It was the best of times, it was the wurst of times." You can correct the wrong letter this way: "It was the best of times, it was the w[o]rst of times."

Any other departures should be indicated with [brackets] or ellipses.

When you quote prose, of course, the line breaks of the original will change to suit your own typeface and margins. When you quote poetry, however, you have to preserve the line breaks and the capitalization of the original. There are two ways to do this: either use a BLOCK QUOTATION that preserves the original lineation and capitalization—

> My mistress' eyes are nothing like the sun;
> Coral is far more red than her lips' red;
> If snow be white, why then her breasts are dun;
> If hairs be wires, black wires grow on her head

—or, if you choose to run the quotation in the text, use slashes to represent the line breaks: "My mistress' eyes are nothing like the sun;/Coral is far more red than her lips' red;/If snow be white, why then her breasts are dun;/If hairs be wires, black wires grow on her head."

QUOTATIONS INSIDE QUOTATIONS.

As I note in the entry on SINGLE QUOTATION MARKS, the usual rule in American usage is that a quotation gets double quotation marks; a quotation inside a quotation gets single. (And so on, alternating between the two, if you have to go several layers deep—though that runs the risk of becoming confusing.)

In general, though, you don't need to put two sets of quotation marks, one double and one single, when the two quotations are "coterminous"—in other words, when they occupy the same space. Consider this passage from Twain's *Huckleberry Finn*:

> Miss Watson would say, "Don't put your feet up there, Huckleberry"; and "Don't scrunch up like that, Huckleberry—set up straight"; and pretty soon she would say, "Don't gap and stretch like that, Huckleberry—why don't you try to behave?" Then she told me all about the bad place, and I said I wished I was there.

If you're going to quote from this passage in your own writing, and want to include both the narrator's voice and Miss Watson's, you'd do it this way:

> In the first Chapter, Twain tells us that "Miss
> Watson would say, 'Don't put your feet up there,
> Huckleberry.'"

That way you're putting the quotation-within-a-quotation
in single quotes. But suppose you want to quote only Miss
Watson's comment: there's no reason to go two levels deep.
You can do it this way:

> As Twain's Miss Watson says, "Don't put your feet
> up there, Huckleberry."

Not a big deal, but worth knowing about.

QUOTE.

An old-timer's rule, probably on the way out, but I'm still
kinda fond of it: use the word *quote* as a verb: you quote
something, and that something is called a *quotation*. Your
English paper or newspaper article should make good use of
quotations, not quotes.

Race, Racism.

See African American and politically loaded language.

Re.

In a memo it's customary to have a "Re:" line—it comes from Latin *in re*, "on the matter of." At the top of a memo, where space is at a premium, it makes sense. But you should avoid using *re* where *concerning*, *regarding*, or *about* will do the trick, as in "*Re* your memo of 13 January...." It makes your writing jargony.

Recasting Sentences.

When you're faced with a stylistic problem you can't easily solve, it's often wise to scrap the troublesome sentence and start from scratch, perhaps using a completely different construction. For instance, if you're bothered by a problem with *his* and *her* (see sexist language and the indefinite third person)—"Just as a musician has to be a master of *his or her* instrument, a writer is at *his or her* best when *he or she* has mastered *his or her* linguistic tools" is downright cumbrous—scrap it all, and use something like "Mastery of words is as important to a writer as mastery of an instrument is to a musician." There's nothing wrong with avoiding such problems; he who fights and runs away lives to fight another etc.

Redundancy.

Pay attention to redundant words and phrases, as in *actual reality* and *anticipate for the future*. Is *advance planning* different from plain old *planning*?—is there any *gift* that's not a *free gift*? See different.

Relative Pronouns.

See pronouns and that *versus* which.

RÉSUMÉ.

The French word is *résumé*, with two accents. As you'll see in the entry on ACCENTS, when we import foreign words we tend to start by preserving the accents, and then we drop them over time. But if you lose both accents from *résumé* you end up with *resume*, which is already an English word.

Most guides, therefore, tell you to preserve at least the second accent: *resumé*. Using both may strike some readers as a little old-fashioned, but it's certainly not wrong.

REVISION.

The writing process isn't over when you reach the end—it has hardly begun. Pay attention to a maxim often quoted in composition classes: "There is no writing, only rewriting." And that means much more than simple PROOFREADING. You should *always* spend a lot of time revising your work—looking not only for outright GRAMMATICAL errors, but also hunting down WASTED WORDS, improving CLARITY and PRECISION, and working on your TRANSITIONS. I know it pains beginning writers to hear that they have so much work to do, but it's really unavoidable. Not even professional writers get it all right in the first draft, so you should be prepared to put as much energy into revision as you do into the original composition.

A tip: let some time pass between your first draft and your revision. That means you have to start putting things on paper well before the deadline. Don't worry: it needn't be perfect; just *write*. And then *forget about it*—for as long as you can afford. (The Roman poet Horace suggested taking a nine-year break between composition and publication, but few professors, bosses, or publishers offer extensions that long.) When you come back to it, you'll be able to read your own writing with fresh eyes, and to see things you missed before. It makes all the difference in the world, but you have to start well before your deadline.

Mind you, it's bad faith for me to pontificate on the moral turpitude of the procrastinator: I'm one of the worst offenders. Do as I say, not as etc.

RHETORIC.

Though *rhetoric* is usually a dirty word in twenty-first-century America, a synonym for "empty words without meaning," I'm determined to reclaim the word—or, if not the word, then at least the idea. It originally referred to the art of persuasion with words.

See AUDIENCE, which is just an expansion of the ideas in this entry.

RHETORICAL QUESTIONS.

Are rhetorical questions ever useful? Yes, they are. Are they, however, grievously overused? Yes indeed. Do they contribute anything to conversation? Almost never. And do I think they're worst when politicians and other dimwits ask themselves what they think? Without a doubt. Do I think the level of public discourse would be raised if the aforementioned dimwits would lose this annoying verbal tic? Absolutely.

RULES.

They ain't a rule in the language what can't be broke. The so-called rules of English GRAMMAR and STYLE were not spoken by a burning bush; they're just guidelines about what's likely to be *effective*. If you learn to treat them that way, you'll live a happier life. To that end, read my entry on PRESCRIPTIVE *VERSUS* DESCRIPTIVE GRAMMARS.

Here's how to think about your task in writing. Step one: figure out where your AUDIENCE is now. Step two: figure out where you want your audience to end up. Step three: take them from one to the other. If you can pull it off, anything goes.

Does that mean all the entries in this guide are superfluous? Not at all. The question is *how* you can drag your audience from one to the other—an audience filled with people of widely varied knowledge, backgrounds, and prejudices. You don't get to pick what hangups your readers suffer from: you have to take them as they are. Writing is an inescapably psychological game, since you have to crawl inside your readers' heads and figure out what's likely to have the desired effects on them.

That's where the rules come in: they're attempts to lay out systematically the effect certain usages will have on certain audiences. A rule that says "Don't SPLIT AN INFINITIVE" can be translated, "*If* you split an infinitive, *then* at least part of your audience will think less of you, and you're less likely to win them over." If you break these rules without a good reason, you lose your audience. It's that simple.

Rules are tools. Don't think of them as bureaucratic regulations designed to get in your way, and don't think of the chance to bend them as a special treat. Instead, think of them as a collection of techniques that are likely to have the desired effect on your readers.

A corollary: there's no single set of rules. Every style, every genre, has its own guidelines. A Nobel Prize speech demands a different style than an MTV Music Awards speech (to my knowledge, the former has never included the word "dudes," nor the latter the word "ineluctable"). Most of the guidelines I lay down here are appropriate for college English papers, a genre calling for a middling degree of FORMALITY—that's also roughly the level that most business communication should have. Other styles have other rules, and all you can do is learn what works in what genre. Keep your AUDIENCE constantly in mind, and learn to *use* the rules—even the ones you find silly—to win them over.

The one unbreakable rule: *Whatever works works.* All that's left for you is to figure out what works. Most of us will spend our lifetimes on that puzzle, and the so-called rules are the closest thing we have to a solution.

See also ACADEMIES, AUDIENCE, PRESCRIPTIVE *VERSUS* DESCRIPTIVE GRAMMARS, and TASTE.

RUN-ON SENTENCES.

Just as there's nothing inherently wrong with a LONG WORD, there's nothing wrong with a long sentence, but it has to be grammatical. A *run-on sentence* is ungrammatical, not just long. It often happens when two sentences are run into one without the proper subordination or punctuation. Independent clauses can't just sit next to each other like that: they need to be either two separate sentences (separated either by a period or a semicolon), or you need a conjunction to separate them.

Two sentences glued together with only a comma produce a COMMA SPLICE, a kind of run-on: for instance, "The semester runs through April, the break begins in May." There are a number of ways of fixing this comma-splice: "The semester runs through April. The break begins in May"; "The semester runs through April, and the break begins in May"; "The semester runs through April; the break begins in May"; "The semester runs through April, whereas the break begins in May," and so on. See SEMICOLON and DEPENDENT *VERSUS* INDEPENDENT CLAUSES.

Examples:

Wrong: Her temperature is over 101 degrees, it just keeps rising.

Right: Her temperature is over 101 degrees; it just keeps rising.

or

Her temperature is over 101 degrees, and it just keeps rising.

Saxon Words.

See Latinate *versus* Germanic diction.

Scientific Writing.

Every field has its own set of professional writing norms, ranging from trivial matters of HOUSE STYLE to much grander notions of what constitutes good and bad writing. Virtually all the advice in this guide is aimed at those writing for a general audience, but it's worth pausing for a moment to consider one important specialized field.

Because medical journals often have to refer to things like "Dihomo-gamma-linolenic acid," they often resort to abbreviations like DGLA—abbreviations that can grow dense and forbidding to the nonspecialist. Because scientists often deal with numbers larger or smaller than the rest of us, they follow different rules for expressing amounts: where a newspaper might write "1.4 million," a scientific journal might write "1.43×10^7."

The demands of science can also have an effect on grammar and style. Much scientific writing, for instance, strives to be impersonal, with the result that the PASSIVE VOICE, usually avoided in writing for a general audience, is actually preferred. In a lab report, for instance, it's traditional to write "50 mg of salt was added," not "We added 50 mg of salt": it doesn't matter *who* did the experiment; what matters is the results.

Scientific writers should still pay attention to much of the advice in this guide: precision is, if anything, even more important in scientific writing than in most other varieties, and if it's possible to avoid long and complicated words without any loss of precision, then you should do it. But remember that every field has its own expectations and conventions; when you're writing for scientists, you play by their rules.

See also JOURNALISM and LEGAL WRITING.

SCOTLAND.

The adjective for people and things from Scotland is *Scottish*; *Scots* is a widely used variant. Don't use *Scotch* except for whiskey and tape. The noun for the inhabitants is *Scots* or *the Scottish*. See also BRITAIN.

SECOND PERSON.

See PERSON.

SELF.

See MYSELF.

SEMICOLONS.

Semicolons probably produce more confusion and misery than all the other punctuation marks combined. But they're really not all that difficult to master.

The semicolon has only two common uses. The first is to separate the items in a list, often after a COLON, especially when the listed items contain commas: "The following books will be covered on the midterm: the *Odyssey*, through book 12; Ovid's *Metamorphoses*, except for the passages on last week's quiz; and the selections from Chaucer." The semicolon makes it clear that there are three items, whereas using commas to separate them could produce confusion.

The other legitimate use of a semicolon is to separate two independent clauses in one sentence: "Shakespeare's comedies seem natural; his tragedies seem forced." We usually use it in cases where the two parts of a sentence are balanced somehow. Here's how to tell whether this one is appropriate: if you can use a period and begin a new sentence, you can use a semicolon. In other words, this kind of semicolon can *always* be replaced by a period and a capital letter. In the example, "Shakespeare's comedies seem natural. His tragedies seem forced" is correct, so a semicolon can be used. (If you used a comma here—"Shakespeare's comedies seem natural, his tragedies seem forced"—you'd be committing the sin of COMMA SPLICE.)

It's risky to use semicolons anywhere else. There's no need for them after, for instance, "Dear Sir" in a letter (where a comma or a colon is preferred). Don't use them before a relative PRONOUN ("She sold more than 400 CDs; which was better than she hoped")—it should be a comma, since the bit after the semicolon can't stand on its own. If you use a semicolon where a comma is more appropriate, you're producing a kind of SENTENCE FRAGMENT.

Examples:

Wrong: An explosion at the nuclear plant would mean the end of life as we know it; which would be a bad thing.

Right: An explosion at the nuclear plant would mean the end of life as we know it, which would be a bad thing.

or

An explosion at the nuclear plant would mean the end of life as we know it, and that would be a bad thing.

SENTENCE.

A sentence should contain *one* idea, though that can be a complex or compound idea. The most obscure sentences in academic writing are sentences filled to bursting. If your writing lacks CLARITY, check to see if a long, bad sentence might make two short, good ones.

This isn't to say that all sentences should be short. Long sentences add variety, and some ideas are too complicated to fit into seven words. The secret is to mix long and short sentences. Too many short, choppy sentences in a row are just as bad as too many long, tortuous sentences in a row. The more you vary sentence length and structure—throwing in some rambling, periodic sentences, and using subordinating conjunctions with dependent clauses (things beginning with *although, because,* and so on)—the more effective your prose will become.

But don't turn your simple ideas into monstrous sentences, devouring line after line without mercy.

SENTENCE FRAGMENTS.

A sentence fragment is a group of words passing itself off as a sentence without having a subject and a verb. Like this. To be avoided.

Some fragments—obviously intentional. A habit picked up from advertising. Not for FORMAL WRITING, unless you're consciously flouting the "rules."

Others are inadvertent, and these require extra care. Pay particular attention to DEPENDENT CLAUSES beginning with relative PRONOUNS like *which* or *who*: they need a proper subject, not a relative pronoun.

SERIAL COMMA.

See COMMAS.

SEX.

See GENDER.

SEXIST LANGUAGE AND THE INDEFINITE THIRD PERSON.

The movement away from sexist language has been a mixed blessing. It has replaced obviously exclusionary terms like *workman's compensation* with *worker's compensation*, but it has also replaced *waiter* or *waitress* with abominations such as *waitperson* or, heaven help us, *waitron* (I feel ill).

It's usually not difficult to be inclusive in your writing, and most of the time a little sensitivity is all it takes to get the job done. It now looks old-fashioned to refer to humanity as "man," or to refer to people generally as "men"; more common now is *humanity* or *people* or some such. That's an easy change to make.

The most confusing problem, though, is the use of the third-person indefinite PRONOUN, as in "Each student is responsible for revising *his/her/their/one's* papers." Which pronoun is correct? It's a delicate question, and no solution is perfect.

Each student is singular—the *is* instead of *are* proves it—so the colloquial *their* (a PLURAL) doesn't AGREE with the verb, and is frowned on by traditionalists. It's common enough in speech—"A friend of mine called me." "What did *they* say?"— but, although many writers have used it, it often sets off alarm bells among many readers of FORMAL WRITING today.

There is an *indefinite* third-person pronoun, *one*, which was once more common than it is now. It helped out in certain situations, but to modern American ears "One should do this" sounds too much like British royalty. It has therefore fallen out of general informal use. There's a place for it in college and business writing, but its usage can be complicated, and I haven't the time to get into the details here. If you're not confident, I suggest you avoid *one*.

Some people now advocate a new set of gender-neutral personal pronouns: favorite sets are *sie*, *hir*, and *hirs*; *zie*, *zir*, and *zirs*; and *ey*, *em*, *eir*, and *eirs*. I confess I find such NEOLOGISMS merely irritating. Besides, readers who haven't yet acquired the secret decoder ring will have no idea what *zirs* means.

…Leaving *his* and *her*, or some combination of the two. "Each student is responsible for revising *his* papers" is the traditional usage, and assumes the masculine pronoun stands for everyone. To many readers, though, it suggests male chauvinism. "Each student is responsible for revising *her* papers" is another possibility, though it can sound patronizing (matronizing?) and seem to beat the reader over the head. "Each student is responsible for revising *his or her* papers" or "*his/her* papers" are both grammatical and nonsexist, but can become clumsy after fifteen or twenty appearances (and see SLASHES).

There are several ways out. I usually opt for *his or her*, and do what I can to keep the extra words from being intrusive. Some prefer to mix the occasional *his or her* together with *his*'s and *her*'s separately; this cuts down on suggestions of sexism without making your writing clumsy. Another is to use *his* sometimes, *her* at other times, although this doesn't feel natural to most writers (yet), and runs the risk of confusing readers. Finally, you can avoid the problem altogether and make your subject plural whenever possible: "*All* students *are* responsible for revising *their* papers." (There's nothing wrong with RECASTING A SENTENCE to dodge a problem.)

My advice: avoid *their* with singular subjects in FORMAL WRITING, and shy away from *his/her* (see SLASHES). *His or her* is probably the best solution, although you should work hard to avoid clumsiness.

See EACH and EVERY for singular nouns that require attention, and POLITICALLY LOADED LANGUAGE for more general advice on sticky topics like this.

SHALL *VERSUS* WILL.

An old distinction, more common in British than in American English, still comes up from time to time. To wit: *will* is usually the simple future indicative: "This *will* happen," "You *will* be surprised." *Shall* is related to the SUBJUNCTIVE, and means "Let it be so," which you might see in LEGAL or business writing: "The employee *shall* produce all required documentation," "A committee *shall* be appointed," and so forth. (They're not just predicting that the employee's going to do it or the committee is going to form; they're declaring that they *must*, or at least *should*, happen.) But this rule works only for the second person (*you*) and the third person (*he, she, it, they*). The first person—*I* and *we*—reverses the rule, so "I *shall* do it" means I'm going to get around to it, while "I *will* do it" shows a mustering of resolve (let it be so).

A favorite example to clarify the two: "I *shall* drown, no one *will* save me!" is a cry of despair, simply predicting imminent death—both are simple futures. "I *will* drown, no one *shall* save me!" is a suicide vow, a declaration that no one had better try to stop me.

I know, it's confusing, but it's nothing to worry about. Just don't throw *shall* around unless you know what you're doing.

SHIBBOLETHS.

And now bow your heads for a reading from the Book of Judges:

> And the Gileadites took the passages of Jordan before the Ephraimites: and it was so, that when those Ephraimites which were escaped said, Let me go over; that the men of Gilead said unto him, Art thou an Ephraimite? If he said, Nay; Then said they unto him, Say now Shibboleth: and he said Sibboleth: for he could not frame to pronounce it right. Then they took him, and slew him at the passages of Jordan. (Judges 12:5–6)

The original *shibboleth* was an arbitrary word that Jephthah used to spot his enemies (it meant either "ear of grain" or "stream"): the Ephraimites had trouble with the *sh* sound and, when asked to pronounce a word with *sh* in it, they revealed they were enemy spies. I suspect few readers of this guide are Ephraimites eager to avoid Gileadite detection, but the story has some modern relevance. The shibboleth provides a handy way to think about language in general.

In its modern sense, a *shibboleth* is some mannerism, usually linguistic, that reveals your origins—and usually without your being aware of it. Some, like the original shibboleth, are matters of pronunciation. It's easy to spot many of the broad differences between American and English accents, but countless little variations are caught only by the most careful listeners. Most Americans, for instance, tend to pronounce the word *been* as if it were *bin*, whereas the English (and other Brits and many Canadians) tend to say *bean*. Americans tend to vocalize the letter *t* between vowels, pronouncing *latter* as if it were *ladder*; in Britspeak the two are clearly different. When Americans try to do English accents (and vice versa), they often miss these little details.

Shibboleths can distinguish not only nationalities but regions. In a Hitchcock movie (I'm dashed if I can remember which) a plot point depends on the pronunciation of the word *insurance*: emphasizing the first syllable rather than the second is characteristic of the American South. The so-called "*pin-pen* vowel" can identify someone from southern Ohio, central Indiana, Illinois, Missouri, Kansas, or Texas. I grew up in southern New Jersey, and can spot fellow south Jerseyans by their pronunciation of *water*, which sounds to the rest of the world like *wooder*.

Other shibboleths are matters of DICTION. STANDARD ENGLISH doesn't distinguish singular *you* from plural *you*, but many regional dialects do. *Y'all* is an obvious give-away of someone from the South and *youse* is common in the New York area; less well known are *y'uns* or *yinz* in Pittsburgh and *yiz* around Philadelphia. The name you use for a long sandwich with various kinds of meats and cheeses—*hoagie, hero, sub, grinder, poorboy*—will similarly reveal where you grew up. (I'm grossly oversimplifying here; linguists like William Labov have done extensive work on many of these topics.)

Shibboleths reveal your background, but that doesn't have to mean location: linguistic habits can also give away your level of education, your profession, your age, your class, and so on. For instance, I'm the sort of hyper-educated dweeb who actually uses *whom* in conversation, and I'd stand no better chance than an Ephraimite if I tried to fit in at a working-class bar. Frequent use of *LIKE* as a verbal tic says you're probably young-ish. Whether you say *pro-life* or *anti-abortion* probably gives away your political position.

Most of these shibboleths evolved by accident, but some are specifically designed to exclude outsiders. It's impossible for me to say *gangsta rap* without sounding like a dork: that's one of the reasons the phrase exists, to mark people like me as outsiders. Quickly changing SLANG is another way of distinguishing the sheep from the goats. By the time I've heard some hip new word or phrase, it's almost certainly obsolete among those who started using it—*phat*, for instance, is on its way to joining *groovy* and *the bee's knees*.

The moral of all this? Most traces of regional pronunciation disappear in writing, of course, but plenty of other kinds of shibboleths shine through. A cautious writer will be conscious of the things most people miss, and use them to his or her advantage. The more attention you pay to others' language and your own, the more sensitive you'll be to these little markers that reveal things about you. The more sensitive you are, the more you'll know about how they affect your AUDIENCE.

Ask yourself: do I want to be perceived as the sort of person who says *ain't* or *insofar as?*—are readers more or less likely to pay attention to me if I refer to *the proletariat?*—do I want people to think I'm from a certain region, of a certain class, of one political persuasion or the other? Once you begin tuning in to the things language reveals, you'll find countless little ways to make your writing more effective.

See also POLITICALLY LOADED LANGUAGE.

Sic.

Apart from necessary omissions and INTERPOLATIONS, your QUOTATIONS should always be exact, and any departures from the original should be clearly indicated with ELLIPSES or brackets.

Sometimes, though, you may have to quote something that looks downright wrong. In these cases, it's traditional to signal to your readers that the oddities are *really* in the original, and not your mistake. The signal is "[*sic*]": square brackets for an interpolation, and the LATIN word *sic*, "thus, this way." (Since it's a foreign word, it's always in italics; since it's a whole word and not an abbreviation, it gets no period.) It amounts to saying, "It really *is* this way, so don't blame me."

George Eliot was a woman: if someone you quote gets it wrong, as in "George Eliot's late fiction shows major advances over his earlier works," you might signal it thus: "George Eliot's late fiction shows major advances over his [*sic*] earlier works." Old spellings were often variable: if your source spells the name *Shakspear*, you might point out with a [*sic*] that it really appears that way in the original.

Don't use *sic* to show off with *gotcha*s. Too many writers sic *sic*s on the authors they quote just to show they spotted a trivial error. If your AUDIENCE is unlikely to be confused, don't draw attention to minor booboos.

SINGLE QUOTATION MARKS.

In general American USAGE, all quoted material goes in "double quotation marks"; if you need a QUOTATION INSIDE A QUOTATION, use 'single quotation marks' (also called "inverted commas") inside: "This for quotations, 'this' for quotations inside quotations."

There are a few fields—philosophy and linguistics among them—where 'single quotation marks' are used for special technical purposes. Unless you're working in one of those fields, though, quotations inside quotations are the *only* place for single quotation marks—don't use them to highlight individual words or to draw attention to figurative expressions, SLANG, or nonstandard usage.

SINGULAR *THEY*.

See SEXIST LANGUAGE AND THE INDEFINITE THIRD PERSON.

SKUNKED TERMS.

File this one under "things I wish I'd made up." The phrase *skunked term* comes from Bryan A. Garner's *Dictionary of Modern American Usage* (New York: Oxford Univ. Press, 1998). Garner describes it this way:

> When a word undergoes a marked change from one use to another…it's likely to be the subject of dispute. Some people (Group 1) insist on the traditional use; others (Group 2) embrace the new use….Any use of [the word] is likely to distract some readers. The new use seems illiterate to Group 1; the old use seems odd to Group 2. The word has become "skunked."

The example he uses is HOPEFULLY (in the sense of "I hope," as in "Hopefully it won't rain"). There are plenty of arguments for it and just as many arguments against it, but if you use it, someone's going to balk, and you're likely to have trouble with your AUDIENCE. Garner adds this advice: "To the writer or speaker for whom credibility is important, it's a good idea to avoid distracting *any* readers or listeners." Lemme get an *amen* from the choir.

SLANG.

Defining slang is notoriously difficult—linguists work in vain to offer a coherent definition that covers everything most people recognize as slang. It's not the same as JARGON, since jargon can be used in formal contexts. It can be obscene or profane, but it needn't be. Although slang words always begin as nonstandard, some eventually make it into standard usage—*cool*, for instance, is still informal, but extremely widespread. Most slang, though, is spoken by a small community. In fact one of the functions of slang is to exclude outsiders (see SHIBBOLETHS): it's a way for hipsters to recognize one another, and to spot potential intruders. I hesitate to introduce examples of contemporary slang for fear that, by the time I've heard of them, they're ridiculously out-of-date in the real world.

But while a precise definition is hard to come by, we can make some generalizations. By its very nature, slang is not the FORMAL variety of STANDARD ENGLISH. It tends to be used in informal contexts, and dropping a slang word or expression into more elevated writing will tend to lower its dignity. This isn't to say you can never use slang. Of course it makes good sense when you're recording dialogue. Even in more formal writing, it can sometimes be effective to drop a slang word or two into your prose to catch readers' attention. You should do it, though, with extreme care, and only if you can be confident your reader knows that you're doing it knowingly.

If you do choose to use slang in formal writing, there's no need to put the words in quotation marks, whether single or double.

That's a clumsy way of drawing attention to your writing. Better to let the tone convey the meaning.

SLASHES.

Slashes are far too common in most writing, and they often betray a lazy thinker: by yoking two words together with a slash, the writer tells us the words are related, but he or she doesn't know exactly how. Whenever possible, replace the slash with *and* or *or*. In a phrase such as "Gulliver encounters people much bigger/smaller than he is," write "Gulliver encounters people much bigger or smaller than he is." Instead of *his/her*, write *his or her*. Find the right conjunction. See AND/OR.

By the way: this / is a slash; this \ is a backslash. Don't confuse them.

SMILEYS.

See EMOTICONS.

SNEAK, SNEAKED, SNUCK.

The traditional past-tense form of *sneak* is *sneaked*, not *snuck*. In FORMAL WRITING, it's probably best to stick with the traditional form, however widespread *snuck* has become in speech.

Here's what *The American Heritage Book of English Usage* has to say:

> The past tense *snuck* is an American invention. It first appeared in the 19th century as a nonstandard regional variant of *sneaked*. But widespread use of *snuck* has become more common with every generation. It is now used by educated speakers in all regions. Formal written English is more conservative than other varieties, of course, and here *snuck* still meets with much resistance. Many writers and editors have a lingering unease about the form, particularly if they recall its nonstandard origins. In fact, in 1990 a review of our citations, exhibiting almost 10,000 instances of *sneaked* and

snuck, indicated that *sneaked* was preferred by a factor of seven to two. And 67 percent of the Usage Panel disapproved of *snuck* in our 1988 survey. Nevertheless, an examination of recent sources shows that *snuck* is sneaking up on *sneaked*. *Snuck* is almost 20 percent more common in newspaper articles published in 1995 than it was in 1985.

Make of that what you will. See also DIVE, DIVED, DOVE.

So.

Avoid using *so* as an intensifier, as in "It's *so* hot," unless there's a *that* clause (though the word *that* needn't actually appear in less formal writing): "It's so hot that the asphalt is melting," "It's so hot I'm thinking of moving to Siberia." *So* on its own, where *very* would be more appropriate, is a low-grade no-no.

So as to.

Often the word *to* will do the trick all by itself.

Solution.

A favorite CLICHÉ of advertisers. *Everything* they want to sell you—every product, every service, every meaningless warm-and-fuzzy feeling of brand identification—is a *solution*. Bleah. And of course it's often paired up with one of my least favorite adjectives, QUALITY, to produce the almost perfectly vapid collocation "quality solutions." It's hard to imagine how you could pack more nonsense into a mere six syllables.

A few years ago I published an article where I groused about that phrase; at the time, a Google search turned up 12,948 examples on the Web. Today the figure stands at more than 1.2 million. I can only assume my rant didn't have its desired effect. As Gulliver writes to his cousin Sympson:

> Instead of seeing a full Stop put to all Abuses and Corruptions, at least in this little Island, as I had Reason to expect: Behold, after above six Months Warning, I cannot learn that my Book hath produced one single Effect according to mine

> Intentions. . . . It must be owned that seven Months
> were a sufficient Time to correct every Vice and
> Folly to which *Yahoos* are subject, if their Natures
> had been capable of the least Disposition to Virtue
> or Wisdom.

Maybe in another six or seven months the world will see things my way.

SPECIES.

The PLURAL is *species*, same as the singular.

SPELLING CHECKERS.

The spelling checkers built into most word processors leave a lot to be desired, but they're not all bad. Whereas GRAMMAR CHECKERS tend to give at least as much bad advice as good, spelling checkers are usually right when they tell you a word is misspelled (only names and rare words are likely to be stopped incorrectly). You should probably turn off the "autocorrect" feature in your word processor, since it tends to make a mess, but otherwise there's little to worry about with things like that.

The big problem, though, isn't false *positives*, but false *negatives*—when the spelling checker tells you something is right when it isn't. If you type *to* instead of *too*, the spelling checker will let it slip right through, since both are legitimate words. Typos are merely venial sins, but if you have any question about the meaning or usage of a word, use a real dictionary, not a spelling checker.

So there's nothing wrong with using a spelling checker to spot slips of the fingers. Just remember that a computerized spelling checker doesn't absolve you from the need to PROOFREAD everything carefully. See also GRAMMAR CHECKERS and MICROSOFT WORD.

SPLIT INFINITIVE.

An INFINITIVE is the form of a VERB that comes after *to*, as in *to support* or *to write*; it's the "uninflected" or base form of the verb (see INFLECTION). A split infinitive—a favorite BUGBEAR of the traditionalists—occurs when another word comes between the *to* and the verb. Adverbs are the worst offenders; they often insinuate themselves between the *to* and the verb, as in "*To boldly go* where no man has gone before," or "*To always keep* a watch on your bag."

Some people prefer to keep the *to* next to the verb at all time and, although authorities are divided over this RULE, it's probably better to avoid split infinitives whenever possible. They're not really *wrong*, but as a matter of style, they can be distracting, and it's better to avoid them whenever you can do it gracefully. Try moving the adverb before the *to* or after the verb; if that fails, consider rewriting the sentence. Instead of "Matt seems *to always do* it that way," try "Matt *always* seems *to do* it that way."

Don't let split infinitives become an obsession; there are times when split infinitives are clearer or more GRACEFUL than their ostensibly more grammatical cousins. See PRESCRIPTIVE *VERSUS* DESCRIPTIVE GRAMMARS and RULES.

Examples:

Disputed: We'd like to more fully consider the question before answering.
Promise to never do that again.

Preferred: We'd like to consider the question more fully before answering.
Promise never to do that again.

STANDARD ENGLISH.

When most people talk about "correct English," they're really talking about one *kind* of English. English comes in countless varieties, and none of them is any more "right" or "proper" than another, at least in the abstract. But one variety has been singled out as the "preferred" form of the language, and that's the one you're taught in school.

That "preferred" form, what linguists call "Standard English" (often abbreviated SE), is the form associated with educated users of the language. Actually, there's not even a single

Standard English, since different countries and different regions have their own standards, and linguists have a dickens of a time even coming up with a good definition of the term. But it's what's expected in college writing, in business writing, and in most newspapers and magazines.

Why is this one variety of English expected in all these places? That's a bigger question than I can answer, and it's the subject of many books. The emergence of SE took centuries, and it's bound up with the history of class structures, educational systems, regional and national prejudices, even race relations— it's a *huge* question. Let the sociolinguists worry about *why* it's expected; it's enough for you to know that it *is* expected, and that if you want to get ahead in these fields, you have to master it.

SE isn't the same as FORMAL English—it's possible to be informal in SE. (Most of this guide is in a casual variety of Standard English.) But most of the RULES you've been taught emerge from descriptions of SE: don't use LIKE as a conjunction, avoid DOUBLE NEGATIVES, distinguish FEWER FROM LESS, and use WHOM as the objective form of *who*. All of these are SHIBBOLETHS that reveal whether you have the "right" sort of background. Since success in college, in business, and in many other fields depends on your convincing people you have that background, it's in your interest to learn SE.

Note that, by some definitions, SE is predominantly a *written* language—and, to be fair, virtually no one speaks "correct" Standard English all the time. Scripted speech on television news programs may come close, and people who speak with great care can sometimes approximate the standard. But spontaneous and informal speech rarely lives up to the expectations of Standard English. Even people who pride themselves on speaking properly are shocked when they see a transcript of their own casual conversation; when they see their own words written down, they think they look like mouth-breathing morons incapable of stringing two words together. But spoken and written English are different things, and in informal speech we make plenty of allowances for things we wouldn't excuse in writing.

This is one of the main reasons why good writers are always good readers: people don't *hear* SE spoken around them, and so the only way to learn it is by *reading* a lot of SE. You can't become proficient in the language unless you're immersed in it.

See also FORMAL WRITING, PRESCRIPTIVE *VERSUS* DESCRIPTIVE GRAMMARS, and RULES.

STATES.

In my experience, the verb *states* is being used more and more often as a SYNONYM for *says* or *writes*—"'The problem,' Thomson states, 'is in the raw materials'"—and that's fine. But *states* is not an exact synonym for either of the other words. Use it only when what you quote is a *statement*—that is, a declarative clause. It doesn't work with questions, with imperatives (that is, commands), or with parts of a sentence; it has to be a full clause that *states* something is happening.

Examples:

Disputed: "Call me Ishmael," Melville states.
"Who are *you?*" stated the Caterpillar.

Preferred: "Call me Ishmael," Melville writes.
"Who are *you?*" asked the Caterpillar.

STORY.

See NOVEL.

STYLE.

Style means all kinds of things. At its grandest, it means everything about your way of presenting yourself in words, including GRACE, CLARITY, and a thousand undefinable qualities that separate good writing from bad. At its narrowest, it includes MECHANICS and matters of HOUSE STYLE.

SUBJUNCTIVES.

Anyone who has studied a foreign language will be glad that English has almost entirely lost the subjunctives it once had. And because English has so few INFLECTIONS, it's often hard to spot the few subjunctives that survive. It's not easy to define the subjunctive; don't worry if you don't follow.

Unlike the *indicative* MOOD, which *indicates* that something is true, the *subjunctive* expresses a wish, a command, or a condition contrary to fact. Archaic English is full of subjunctives, as in "Would that it were" and "Thou shalt not."

The English subjunctive still shows up in a few places, of which the condition contrary to fact is most common:

>**Conditions contrary to fact:** "If I *were* a rich man." (I teach English; Lord knows I ain't rich.) We use *were* instead of the expected *is*, *am*, or *are*: "If this *were* any heavier [but it's not—a condition contrary to fact], I couldn't lift it"; "If she *were* to say that [but she's not], I'd leave."
>
>**Suppositions:** "If I *were* to tell you, I'd have to kill you"; "*Be* that as it may."
>
>**Wishes:** "I wish I *had* an Illudium PU-36 Explosive Space Modulator"; "I wish she *were* six inches taller."
>
>**Demands and suggestions:** "I insisted that he *leave*"; "I suggested he *leave*."
>
>**Necessity or importance:** "It's essential that he *arrive* on time."

Some also classify *shall* as a subjunctive (see SHALL VERSUS WILL).

SUBSTANTIVE.

Substantive is the technical term for a word or group of words acting as a NOUN. Since modern GRAMMAR is more concerned with the way words function in a sentence than with PART-OF-SPEECH designations in a dictionary, it's a little different from the conventional understanding of *noun*, but it's close. Virtually all nouns are substantives; so are PRONOUNS like *he*, *she*, *it*, and *they*. It can also include ADJECTIVES if they're used "absolutely"—*the homeless*, for instance, or *the wicked*.

SUPERSCRIPT.

Don't let your word processor force superscripts—that is, small letters above the baseline of the text—where they don't belong. MICROSOFT WORD introduced a feature that automatically converts the letters in ordinal numbers (the *st* in *1st*, the *nd* in *2nd*, the *rd* in *3rd*, and so on) into superscripts: not *1st* but *1ˢᵗ*; not *2nd* but *2ⁿᵈ*; not *3rd* but *3ʳᵈ*. Turn it off. Use superscript numbers for footnote and endnote references; reproduce any superscripts that appear in material you're quoting—otherwise you can comfortably do without the feature altogether.

SYNONYMS.

Synonym means "the same meaning"; it's used to refer to pairs (or trios, or whatever) of words that are interchangeable. But here's the rub: no two words in the language are perfectly interchangeable. Even when their denotations are letter-for-letter the same, their CONNOTATIONS will always be a little different: one word might be informal and another formal; one might be jocular and another dead serious; one might have historical associations lacking in another; and so on.

So when we talk about synonyms, we mean words that are *close* in meaning to one another. Still, you have to choose among them carefully. Pay attention to the effect each word might have on your audience, and choose accordingly.

See also CONNOTATION *VERSUS* DENOTATION, DICTION, and THESAURUS.

TASK.

The VERB *to task* (meaning "to impose a task on") has been around a long time: the *Oxford English Dictionary* records the first example in 1530. But geez, it's ugly, innit? Garner dismisses it as a "vogue word" in *A Dictionary of Modern American Usage*; I object because it's a thoughtless CLICHÉ in business writing.

TASTE.

As in "There's no accounting for" (*de gustibus non est disputandum*). Few people want to hear it—we all crave authoritative answers—but taste is part of any discussion of language. The RULES go only so far; after that, all you've got to guide you are preferences.

Me, personally, myself, I'd sooner go to my *grave* than use *disconnect* as a noun ("There's a big disconnect between what he says and what he does"): I feel so *dirty* when I have to say it. The word LIFESTYLE makes my teeth itch, and I'd rather gnaw my own leg off than say something like "ANY WAY, SHAPE, OR FORM." (Ditto phrases like "Me, personally, myself.")

But they're not *right* or *wrong*, and certainly not the sort of thing that a grammar guide can settle definitively: there's no authoritative answer. I find them ugly as sin, but your mileage may vary. They're a matter of taste.

I, of course, am convinced I have *impeccable* taste; and like most people who set up linguistic soapboxes, I sometimes offer opinions on such questions. I like to think I'm rarely perverse or pedantic, and I flatter myself that I have a better ear for style than many. But take my opinions for what they're worth: they're one guy's judgment on what sounds good. And on many issues, that's all you get.

See ACADEMIES, AUDIENCE, BUGBEARS, GRAMMAR, HOUSE STYLE, PRESCRIPTIVE *VERSUS* DESCRIPTIVE GRAMMARS, and STYLE.

TENSE.

Tense is a property of VERBS to indicate *when* an action happened, happens, or will happen. The usual tenses are *past*, *present*, and *future*. With regular verbs, the past tense is usually formed with "-ed" (*walked*); the present tense is the "uninflected" or base form of the verb (*walk*); and the future tense is usually formed with SHALL OR WILL. (Some argue that, because we don't have a separate inflection for the future—we form it with an AUXILIARY VERB—English doesn't really have a future tense. Seems a niggling distinction to me, but what do I know?)

Note that *tense* is sometimes folded together with ASPECT and treated as a single category. By this standard, "simple present" (*I go*) and "continuous present" (*I am going*) are different tenses, as are "simple past" or "preterite" (*I went*), "past continuous" or "imperfect" (*I was going*), and "past perfect" or "pluperfect" (*I had gone*). Others prefer to use *tense* to refer only to time of the action, and treat *aspect* as a separate category.

THAN I *VERSUS* THAN ME.

Than, as used in comparisons, has traditionally been considered a CONJUNCTION; as such, if you're comparing subjects, the PRONOUNS after *than* should take the "subjective CASE." In other words, "He's taller than *I*," not "He's taller than *me*"; "She's smarter than *he*," not "She's smarter than *him*." If, on the other hand, you're comparing direct or indirect objects, the pronouns should be objective: "I've never worked with a more difficult client than *him*."

There are some advantages to this traditional state of affairs. If you observe this distinction, you can be more precise in some comparisons. Consider these two sentences:

He has more friends *than I*. (His total number of friends is higher than my total number of friends.)

He has more friends *than me*. (I'm not his only friend; he has others.)

The problem, though, is that in all but the most FORMAL contexts, "than I" sounds stuffy, even unidiomatic. Most people, in most contexts, treat *than* as a PREPOSITION, and put all following pronouns in the objective CASE, whether the things being compared are subjects or objects. "He's taller *than me*" sounds more natural to most native English speakers.

This isn't a recent development: people have been treating *than* as a preposition for centuries. Consider the following from big-name English and American writers:

> Matthew Prior, *Better Answer*: "For thou art a girl as much brighter than her,/As he was a poet sublimer than me."

> Samuel Richardson's *Clarissa*: "I am fitter for this world than you, you for the next than me."

> Lord Byron's letter of 2 November 1804: "Lord Delawarr is considerably younger than me."

> Robert Southey, *Well of St. Keyne*: "She had been wiser than me,/For she took a bottle to Church."

> William Faulkner's *Reivers*: "Let Lucius get out . . . He's younger than me and stouter too for his size."

So what should you do? I don't have a good answer, other than the most general advice possible: try to size up your AUDIENCE, and figure out whether they're likely to be happier with the traditional or the familiar usage.

THAN *VERSUS* THEN.

Than is a CONJUNCTION or PREPOSITION used in unequal comparisons; *then* is (usually) an adverb indicating time or consequence. Be careful not to CONFUSE them: something is bigger *than* something else; something happens *then*.

Examples:

Wrong: D. H. Lawrence is worse then any other English author.

Right: D. H. Lawrence is worse than any other English author.

THAT *VERSUS* WHICH.

Many guides maintain that the word *that* is restrictive, while *which* is not. Now, this is a little problematic. There isn't much historical justification for the rule, and many of the best writers in the language couldn't tell you the difference between them. If the subtle difference between the two confuses you, you can probably use whatever sounds right without fretting over it too much. Other matters are more worthy of your attention.

For the curious, however, here's the skinny on the traditional distinction. The relative PRONOUN *that* is restrictive, which means it tells you a necessary piece of information about its antecedent: for example, "The word processor *that* is used most often is Word." Here the *that* phrase answers an important question: which of the many word processors are we talking about? And the answer is the one that is used most often.

Which is non-restrictive: it does not limit the word it refers to. For example, "The current policy, *which* went into effect in 2004, will soon be phased out." Here *that* is unnecessary: the *which* does not tell us which of the many current policies we're considering; it simply provides an extra piece of information about the policy we're already discussing. "The current policy" tells us all we really need to know to identify it.

It boils down to this: if you can tell which thing is being discussed without the *which* or *that* clause, use *which*; if you can't, use *that*.

There are two rules of thumb you can keep in mind. First, if the phrase needs a comma, you probably mean *which*. Since "The current policy" calls for a comma, we would not say "The current policy, that went into effect in 2004."

Another way to keep them straight is to imagine *by the way* following every *which*: "The current policy, which (by the way) went into effect in 2004 . . . ." The *which* adds a useful, but not grammatically necessary, piece of information. On the other hand, we wouldn't say "The word processor which (by the way) is used most often is Word," because *the word processor* on its own isn't enough information—*which* word processor?

A paradoxical mnemonic: use *that* to tell which, and *which* to tell that.

THEIR, THERE, THEY'RE.

Three words that share a pronunciation. *Their*: belonging to them ("This is their house"). *There*: not here ("It's over there"). *They're*: a CONTRACTION of *they are* ("They're always getting into trouble"). Don't confuse them.

THEIRSELF, THEMSELF.

See MYSELF.

THEREFORE *VERSUS* THEREFOR.

Both are real words and will probably get through your SPELLING CHECKER, but they mean different things. *Therefore* with a final *e* is the much more common word; it means "for that reason" or "consequently." *Therefor* without the final *e* is archaic in most contexts, and today you're likely to see it only in LEGAL documents. It means "for that" (just as *thereto* means "to that" and *therefrom* means "from that"). Unless you're in a law office, you almost certainly want *therefore*.

THESAURUS.

Exercise great care when you use a thesaurus. If you use it only to remind yourself of words you already know, but that don't come to mind immediately, that's fine—an unexpected word can really make a sentence come to life. If you describe a villain as *dastardly*, a wretched bit of prose as *flaccid*, something very light as *gossamer*, or a grumpy person as *churlish*, you can add zing to an otherwise feeble sentence.

Too often, though, people turn to a thesaurus for obscure words they've never seen before. The result is show-offy LONG WORDS and OBFUSCATION, as simple words like *important* get replaced by monstrosities like *exigent, ponderous,* or *importunate* (and none of them is really the same as *important*). Confession time: when I was in seventh grade, I had to write an essay in which I wanted to say (of what I forget) that "We don't want it and we don't need it." Afraid that this wouldn't sound impressive enough, I went to the thesaurus, and ended up with "It is neither necessitous nor desiderative." At the time I thought I was oh-so-clever. Decades have passed since that day, but I still burn in shame.

Better than a standard thesaurus, then, is a dictionary of SYNONYMS, which not only lists related words but explains how they're used and the differences between them. If you choose to stick with a conventional thesaurus, at least be sure you know the meanings of the words you draw from it.

See also DICTIONARIES, DENOTATION *VERSUS* CONNOTATION, and SYNONYMS.

THEY.

See SEXIST LANGUAGE AND THE INDEFINITE THIRD PERSON.

THIRD PERSON.

See PERSON.

THIS.

See ANTECEDENT.

THUSLY.

Thus is already an adverb; it doesn't need a *-ly*.

TITLES.

A heads-up: this entry is about titles of works, not of people. For personal titles (Mr., Mrs., Ms., Sir, Lady, Lord, Rev.), see NAMES.

The titles of books and other long works (plays, long poems, operas, etc.) are either ITALICIZED or underscored; likewise titles of serials (magazines, newspapers, television series). The titles of shorter works (essays, short poems, etc.) appear in quotation marks. For borderline cases, the test is whether it could be published as a book on its own: even if you're reading *King Lear* in a larger anthology, it's long enough that it could be a book, so it gets italics. Don't fret the occasional necessary judgment call; even professional literary scholars sometimes disagree on how to treat some works.

(Note that many newspapers use quotation marks for *all* titles, whether of short or long works. This is because, in the days of lead type, many newspapers didn't have an italic typeface, and it remains the norm even in the age of digital fonts. Other publications, though, use italics or underscore for titles of long works.)

In most HOUSE STYLES, all the major words in an English title are CAPITALIZED—"major" meaning the first word, the last word, and everything in between except ARTICLES, CONJUNCTIONS, and PREPOSITIONS: *A Tale of Two Cities* (preposition *of* gets no cap), "I Have a Dream" (article *a* gets no cap). If there's a subtitle, the same rules apply to the subtitle, even if it begins with an article, conjunction, or preposition: *Authors and Owners: The Invention of Copyright* (conjunction *and* and preposition *of* get no caps, but article *the* is the first word of the subtitle). There are other styles; some publications capitalize only the first word and proper names, and there are different rules for other languages. But it's usually safe to capitalize everything but the articles, conjunctions, and prepositions.

Many guides call for omitting initial ARTICLES in titles if the titles follow a POSSESSIVE: "In his *Tale of a Tub*, Swift satirizes zealots" (the title is *A Tale of a Tub*, but "his *A*" sounds clumsy); "In Ann Radcliffe's *Mysteries of Udolpho*" (the title is *The Mysteries of Udolpho*, but the *the* can go). Another possibility—and sometimes a better one—is to leave out the possessive ("his," "her") when it's unnecessary. When readers see "as Fitzgerald writes in his *Great Gatsby*," there's little chance they'll be confused into thinking Fitzgerald wrote it in someone else's *Great Gatsby*—you can leave out the "his" and use the *The*.

TOTALLY.

See WASTED WORDS.

TOWARD *VERSUS* TOWARDS.

They're interchangeable. *Toward* is a little more common in America, and *towards* a little more common in Britain; but both forms are perfectly acceptable in either place.

TRAGEDY.

Why must everything unpleasant or unfortunate be billed as a *tragedy*?

I'm an English professor; I prefer to limit the word to works of literature, especially dramatic literature, that involve a protagonist (the "tragic hero") suffering a downfall because of some character flaw.

But hey, not everyone wants to be an English professor (*tant pis pour vous*). I won't make too big a fuss if others choose to apply the word to real-life situations rather than the works of Sophocles and Shakespeare. If you want to call the deaths of Anne Frank and José Martí *tragic*, knock yourself out.

I *do* get cranky, though, when people apply it to trivial disappointments. Even many natural disasters—forest fires, say—don't seem to me really *tragic*. They *suck*; they're *disasters*, *calamities*, even *cataclysms* or *catastrophes*; they're *deplorable*, *lamentable*, *pitiful*, *woeful*, maybe even *ineffable*—but the word *tragic* has been used so often it's now either cant or a CLICHÉ. Let's give it a rest, huh?

TRANSITION.

Transition is a perfectly respectable NOUN; it's been in the language since before Shakespeare was born. It's increasingly being used, though, as a VERB—"We'll be *transitioning* to the new system over the next few months"—and that's kinda ugly. It's still fairly recent (the *OED* can trace it back only to 1975), and still sounds JARGONY to most ears. My advice is to avoid it whenever you can.

TRANSITIONS.

Writing should flow. Each sentence should follow on the one before it, and each paragraph should pick up where the previous one left off. Try to make the connections between your sentences and paragraphs logical and explicit. The paragraph's *topic sentence* is a good place for this, and mastery of transitional words and phrases like *therefore, however, on the other hand*, and so forth is a must. See PARAGRAPHS.

TRANSITIVE *VERSUS* INTRANSITIVE VERBS.

A *transitive* verb takes a DIRECT OBJECT: it shows action upon someone or something. An *intransitive* verb takes no direct object; it needs only a subject to make a sentence.

Some transitive verbs: *Hit* (you hit *something* or *someone*; you don't just *hit*); *climb* (you don't just *climb*; you climb *something*); and *bring* (bring *what?*). Intransitive verbs: *sleep* (you don't *sleep something*; you just *sleep*); and *fall* (while you can fall *down* the stairs, you don't *fall the stairs*).

There are a few things worth noticing. First, just because something grammatically needs a direct object doesn't mean we actually use it. If someone said, *I swung the bat and hit*, we don't have to ask *what* he hit; the direct object *ball* is understood.

Second, many intransitives might look like transitives, as in *She walked three hours*. Here *three hours* is not really a direct object; it doesn't say *what* she walked, but *how long* (it's actually an adverbial phrase).

Third, many verbs can be both transitive and intransitive: while a word like *ran* is usually intransitive, it can also be transitive in "He ran the program for two years." Children can *play catch*, or they can just *play*. Even *sleep*, given above as an intransitive, could become transitive if we said *He slept the sleep of the righteous.*

The only real danger is when you start changing verbs willy-nilly: "We have to think quality" (giving the intransitive *think* a direct object; you probably mean "think *about* quality," if you mean anything at all); "I hope you enjoy" (instead of *enjoy it*).

TRANSLITERATION.

It's easy to reproduce words from some foreign languages in English: French *livre*, German *Buch*, Italian and Spanish *libro*, and so on. That's because their alphabets are very close to ours (with a few characters that aren't part of English: French *façade*, German *Schuß*, Spanish *niño*, and so on). Other languages use a more modified Latin alphabet—Polish *stół* or *żeście*, Czech *pět mužů*—but the basic letter shapes are the same, and they're not very difficult to render in English.

Other languages don't use the Latin alphabet at all, and they pose bigger challenges. Switching into the foreign alphabet won't do—you don't usually see Σοφοκλης (Sophocles) or Ленин (Lenin). You have to turn them into our alphabet, the technical term for which is *transliteration*, "moving from one set of letters to another." It's not the same as *translation*; you're not changing the meaning of anything, simply spelling the word in another alphabet. (Another common term is *romanization*, for "moving into the roman alphabet.") Unfortunately, there are competing systems of transliterating many of the world's writing systems. Some preserve features of the original languages but produce a mess that a lay reader can't pronounce without learning the technicalities of the system; others are easy to pronounce but lose the niceties of the original language. And the world's languages use many sounds that simply don't exist in English, which have to be rendered with unfamiliar symbols (apostrophes for glottal stops, digraphs like *ch* for guttural fricatives, exclamation points for !Xung clicks, and so on).

The result is that you may see words and names with various spellings. The holy book of Islam might show up as the *Koran*

or the *Qu'ran*; the name of the Chinese leader was spelled
Mao Tse Tung with the Wade-Giles system but *Mao Zedong*
with pinyin; in Russian you might see the nineteenth-century
Russian author's name as *Dostoevski, Dostoevsky, Dostoyevski,
Dostoyevsky, Dostoievski*, and probably a few others I haven't
thought of. The composer might be *Tchaikovsky, Tchaikowski*,
or *Tchaikowskij*.

How to handle this variety? If you're quoting someone, follow
the original spelling. If you have to pick a form to use yourself,
find out whether one system is preferred in your field (in a
course on Chinese history, for instance, you'll probably be
expected to use pinyin). If there's no clear preference for one
system over another, pick the one that will be recognized by
the widest variety of your readers.

See also MOSLEM *VERSUS* MUSLIM.

TRY AND.

"Try and" is common enough in speech, but it's out of place in
FORMAL PROSE. Use "try to."

Examples:

Informal: Just try and stop me.
Formal: Just try to stop me.

TRYING TO SAY.

It's probably best to eliminate this phrase from your
vocabulary, since it usually adds nothing to a sentence.
Especially if you're writing about major works literature, you
can assume that major authors *did* say exactly what they were
trying to say. Shakespeare, Milton, Austen, Poe, Melville,
Twain, Joyce, Woolf, Ellison—these people make the big
bucks, or at least their ghosts do, because they said exactly
what they meant to say. You might have a reason to take
something they wrote and put it into your own words—see
PARAPHRASE—and that's fine, but remember that's what
you're trying to say, not them. Find a more precise formulation

to introduce your own paraphrase or summary, one that explains exactly how your words are related to your author's.

Use "trying to say" only when you have a good reason to think your author somehow failed to say what he or she meant.

UNCONSCIOUS HABITS.

We all acquire little stylistic tics that we're not always aware of. They can be favorite words, sentence structures, punctuation marks, just about anything. As for me, I never met a semicolon I didn't like—if I had my way, every sentence would have two or three. I'm also too fond of *in fact*, a transition I use whenever I can. But when these eccentricities come too often, they can get on your readers' nerves.

The difficulty is that we're usually not aware of these habits, especially when the writing is still fresh. If enough time goes by, though, you'll be able read what you actually wrote, instead of what you meant to write. It's therefore a good idea to take some time away from something you write and to reread it carefully, looking for habits that you use over and over. Then your last step in the writing process can be to go through each piece and to trim anything you find yourself using too often.

See IDIOLECT and REVISION.

UNDERSCORES.

See ITALICS.

UNINTERESTED *VERSUS* DISINTERESTED.

See DISINTERESTED *VERSUS* UNINTERESTED.

UNDOUBTEDLY.

See CLEARLY, OBVIOUSLY, UNDOUBTEDLY.

UNIQUE.

Unique means "one of a kind"; it's the same *uni-* ("one") as *unicycle* (one wheel) and *unicorn* (one horn). There are no degrees of uniqueness: something is unique, or it is not.

Expressions like "very unique," therefore, are frowned on. If you want a word that admits degrees, use *special, unusual, distinctive,* or something like that.

UNITED KINGDOM.

See BRITAIN.

USAGE.

Usage is a guide on how to use something properly; *use* means "one or more instances of using something," or "function." Thus the *use* of a SEMICOLON is to separate clauses, while its *usage* is the list of RULES on exactly how it has to be used. Someone who knows the *use* of a word understands how it fits in a sentence; someone who knows the *usage* has studied the grammatical rules, semantic relations, and appropriate MECHANICS. Each time you use something, that's one *use* (the noun), not one *usage*. Unless you're talking about grammar, you usually mean *use* rather than *usage*: don't use the longer word just because it sounds more impressive.

USED TO.

We often form the past TENSE, habitual ASPECT, with the AUXILIARY VERB *used to*: "She used to eat at that restaurant," for instance, means it happened in the past, and it happened more than once.

The difficulty comes from that final *-d* in *used*. First, we tend not to pronounce it clearly, leading many people to think it's not there. But you should always write *used to*, not *use to*, at least in the past tense. Second, what happens when you need to change the form of the verb? For instance, suppose you wanted to put the restaurant sentence in the negative: "didn't used to"?—"didn't use to"?

Most guides recommend "didn't use to," letting the auxiliary verb *do* take the past tense (*did*): "She didn't use to eat at that restaurant," "Did she use to eat at that restaurant?"—that sort of thing. That's correct enough, though it strikes many readers as unidiomatic. If it bothers you, consider a different construction altogether: "She never used to eat at that restaurant," "She wouldn't eat at that restaurant," something along those lines.

UTILIZE AND UTILIZATION.

Use is almost always better, whether pronounced *yooz* as a verb or *yoos* as a noun. Don't longwordify what would otherwise be clear.

VERBAL.

Verbal means "related to words"; a written agreement is just as *verbal* as an oral one. Many people use it as the opposite of "written," but there's still a band of brave souls who resist it. If you mean something spoken, use *oral*. Samuel Goldwyn ignored this distinction in his quip, "A verbal agreement isn't worth the paper it's written on."

VERBS.

A *verb* is a PART OF SPEECH that shows *action* or a *state of being*. Some examples: *talk, worry, demonstrate, exist, calibrate*, and *be*.

Note that English is flexible enough to allow many words or phrases to operate as verbs, though most of the new coinages are still considered informal, and a lot of them won't show up in most dictionaries. The noun *pants*, for instance, can become a verb meaning "to pull someone's pants down" (usually as a prank); *to gift* (meaning "to give a gift") was popular some years ago (and became fashionable again when *Seinfeld* coined the verb *to re-gift*); businessfolk are fond of verbs like *to transition* and *to liaise*. I find most of the businessy ones ugly as sin, but they don't violate any "RULES."

If you spot a verb "in the wild," you can classify it according to a number of categories:

The PERSON indicates who or what is doing the action, whether the speaker, the addressee, or someone or something else.

The NUMBER indicates how many people or things are doing the action, whether one or many.

The TENSE indicates the *time* of the action, which can be past, present, or future.

The VOICE indicates whether the subject of the clause is acting or being acted upon.

Active verbs can be either TRANSITIVE OR INTRANSITIVE, that is, they may take a DIRECT OBJECT or they may not.

The ASPECT indicates whether the action was completed, is continuing, starts and stops, and so on.

The MOOD indicates something like the way the action is viewed—whether it actually happened, or might have happened, or should happen, and so on; it can be indicative, subjunctive, conditional, imperative, and so on.

A comprehensive description of a verb would include something on all these categories. Here are the first two sentences of *Moby-Dick*, with more or less full descriptions of the main verbs (which I've italicized) in each clause:

> *Call* me Ishmael.

Call is the IMPERATIVE of an active and TRANSITIVE verb. In English we don't distinguish person, number, or aspect of imperatives, though some languages do.

> Some years ago—never *mind* how long precisely— ...

Another imperative.

> ...*having* little or no money in my purse...

Having is the present PARTICIPLE of the active, indicative, transitive verb *to have*; the present participle indicates a continuing aspect.

> ...and nothing particular *to interest* me on shore...

The INFINITIVE, usually (but not always) spotted by the accompanying particle *to*. *To interest* is an active and transitive verb.

> ...I *thought*...

First person, singular, past tense, active voice, intransitive, completed aspect, indicative mood.

> ...I *would sail* about a little and *see* the watery part of the world.

Here the verbs are *would sail* and *[would] see*: First person, singular, indicative, future tense, active voice, transitive, continuous aspect, subjunctive mood. (Whew!)

The only people who routinely have to break down verbs this obsessively are those learning a foreign language. And I've made no effort to define things precisely; linguists still wrangle over the finer points, and I'm simply not qualified to give the final word on anything. Still, this should offer you a basic understanding of what's going on, and give you the vocabulary to discuss verbs in more detail should you want to do that.

See also ACTION VERBS, LINKING VERBS, and TRANSITIVE *VERSUS* INTRANSITIVE VERBS.

VERY.

See WASTED WORDS.

VIRUS.

Many Latin words ending in *-us* take a PLURAL in *-i*, but this isn't one of them. In fact there is no classical Latin plural for *virus*; it was a mass noun, not a COUNT NOUN, so it didn't take a plural. The modern English plural follows plain old English rules: *viruses*. This applies to the microbe critters of biology and the malicious programs of computer hackers.

For other plurals that seem violate the *us*-to-*i* rule, see APPARATUS, CORPUS, GENIUS, GENUS, and OPUS.

VOCABULARY.

Having a large vocabulary can never hurt, but you should use your energy wisely. Though knowing words like *obnubilate, hebetic,* and *tergiversation* can make you the envy of your crossword-puzzle-playing friends, in writing you'll get more mileage out of knowing the PRECISE meaning of more common words. Can you distinguish *climatic* from *climactic?—tortuous* from *torturous?—incredible* from *incredulous?—turgid* from *turbid*? They're very different, but often CONFUSED. For a good guide, to these pairs and others, see Maxwell Nurnberg in the "Additional Reading" section.

Don't use obscure words just because you can; ostentation leads only to OBFUSCATION. Using *mirific* where *amazing* or *wonderful* will do is just showing off and intimidating your AUDIENCE. See also LONG WORDS and THESAURUS.

VOICE.

Voice is a technical term in GRAMMAR to describe a verb: the common voices in English are *active* and *passive*. Voice describes whether the subject of a sentence is *acting* or *being acted upon*. See PASSIVE VOICE for details.

Wales.

See Britain.

Wasted Words.

Many words and phrases rarely add anything to a sentence. Avoid these whenever you can. A short list of some of the worst offenders: *quite, very, extremely, as it were, moreover, it can be seen that, it has been indicated that, basically, essentially, totally, completely, therefore, it should be remembered that, it should be noted that, thus, it is imperative that, at the present moment in time.* These are fine in their place, but they often slither into your writing with the sinister purpose of tempting you into the sin of padding your sentences. See economy.

Web Site, Web-site, Website, web site, web-site, website.

As with other high-tech neologisms—see E-mail and on-line—there's little agreement over whether the *W* should be capital and whether it should be two words, a hyphenated compound, or one word. It's a matter of house style.

Webster's.

See dictionaries.

Which *versus* That.

See that *versus* which.

Who *versus* That or Which.

You should usually use *who* (and its related forms, *whose* and *whom*) only to refer to people, with *that* or *which* only for non-human things: "a woman *who* lived nearby" (not *that* or *which*); "a concert *that* set attendance records" (not *who*).

The only time it's advisable to use *who*-forms with non-human things is in the *whose* construction: "the cars *that* were built by Ford," but "the cars *whose* tires were made by Firestone." That saves you from the inelegant construction "the cars, the tires *of which* were made by Firestone." Even there, though, it's still a little clumsy; if you can reword it to avoid referring to a thing as *who*, consider doing it.

Examples:

Wrong: Toni Morrison may be the only "literary" author that is also popular with a mass-market readership.

Right: Toni Morrison may be the only "literary" author who is also popular with a mass-market readership.

WHO *VERSUS* WHOM.

While it's possible to memorize a rule for distinguishing *who* from *whom*, it's easier to trust your ear. A simple test to see which is proper is to replace *who/whom* with *he/him*. If *he* sounds right, use *who*; if *him* is right, use *whom*. For example: since *he did it* and not *him did it*, use *who did it*; since we give something *to him* and not *to he*, use *to whom*. It gets messy only when the PREPOSITION is separated from the *who*: *Who/whom did you give it to?* Rearrange the words in your head: "*To whom* did you give it?" See PREPOSITION AT THE END and HYPERCORRECTION.

Examples:

Wrong: The company has to pay restitution to everyone who they injured.

Whom should I say is calling?

Right: The company has to pay restitution to everyone whom they injured.

Who should I say is calling?

Whose *versus* Who's.

A CONFUSING PAIR, like *ITS* AND *IT'S*. *Whose* means "of whom" or "belonging to whom"; *who's* is a CONTRACTION of "who is" or "who has."

Examples:

Wrong:	Who's is it?
	Whose coming to dinner?
Right:	Whose is it?
	Who's coming to dinner?

-Wise.

Ad hoc words like *salarywise* and *timewise*, meaning *regarding* salaries or time, are best avoided. Strunk and White put it well: "The sober writer will abstain from the use of this wild additive."

Wont *versus* Won't.

They're both real words, and will both get past your SPELLING CHECKER, but they mean different things. *Won't* with an apostrophe is the CONTRACTION for *will not*. *Wont* without an apostrophe is much rarer, probably heading for obsolescence, but still used occasionally. It can be an ADJECTIVE meaning "accustomed to" or "likely," as in "He's wont to complain whenever they ask him to do some work." It can also mean "habit" or "custom," as in "It was her wont to stop by the coffee shop on the way home from work."

See also CANT *VERSUS* CAN'T.

A Guide to Citation

WHAT TO CITE

Knowing *how* to cite is important, but let's begin by discussing *what* to cite and *why*.

First, what. Here's the short formulation: if you had to look it up, you have to cite it. That means any direct quotation from a book (or movie or Web site or whatever), however short, should be cited. It also means that any fact you've taken from your reading should be cited. The only exception is "common knowledge"—if something is widely known, you needn't say you read it in any particular source. So, for instance, if you have some reason to point out that February is the shortest month, there's no need to footnote it; virtually everyone knows that. It's usually not necessary to cite encyclopedias or dictionaries for something widely reported in other sources, like the dates of birth and death of an author. But if you quote their exact words, cite them.

How do you know when something is "common knowledge"? If you're in doubt, cite it. Few professors will object to too many citations, but we get grumpy when things that should be cited aren't.

WHY TO CITE

That's what to cite. How about why? It's not just a matter of performing arbitrary gestures to keep your professors happy; citation is serious business. It amounts to putting your intellectual cards on the table. It allows a reader to check your facts, and to follow up your argument by returning to the sources you used. It also shows that you understand what you've read, and that you're not simply regurgitating what you've found.

How to Cite

Now, *how* do you cite something? There are several competing standards; your professor may prefer one over the others, but they're all equally "right." The various disciplines (math, psychology, medicine) have their own styles, but two are common in American English classes, known familiarly as "Chicago style" (named for the *Chicago Manual of Style*) and "MLA style" (named for the Modern Language Association, which publishes the appropriate guidebooks). An instructor will probably recommend one over the other (or may recommend another guide altogether). If you're not told which format to use, though, either of these is a safe bet. The *Chicago Manual* costs a bundle, and owning it is probably out of your league unless you write for a living. But if you're an English major, you should probably pony up the dough for the MLA guide; it's under $20.

Examples of the exact format for citations appear below, but I begin with some general advice that applies to all the style guides.

First, every citation should include all of the following pieces of information, at least whenever they apply:

Full name of the author or authors, as stated on the title page. Don't abbreviate them, though you can omit titles that appear after the names, like "Ph.D." If the work is an anthology or collection of pieces by many people, use the names of the volume editor or editors. If there's a long list of authors or editors—say, more than three—you can list the first few, adding "et al."—"and others"—to the end.

Full title and subtitle of the work—whether a book, an article, an essay, a poem, or whatever. If this is a book-length work, it should be italicized or underscored (see the entry on ITALICS for details). Sometimes it's not easy to figure out exactly what the proper title should be: the cover of the book may say one thing, the spine another, the title page something else again. In cases like this, the "official" version of the title is the one that appears on the full title page (not the so-called "half-title," which often appears before the title page and gives just a short version of the title).

These are close to universal—just about everything you might cite has a creator and a title. Other pieces of information vary, depending on the kind of source.

When you cite *books*, *articles*, or *short stories*, provide the following:

Full name of the editor or editors, if provided. This is for works by a single author that also carry an editor: William Shakespeare, *King Lear*, ed. Stephen Orgel. If the book is an anthology containing pieces by many authors, the editor's name appears first, in place of an author's name.

Edition, if after the first. Note, though, you don't need to worry about multiple printings, only multiple editions. Specify the edition as it appears on the title page or in the copyright information: if it says "second edition," you cite it as "2nd ed."; if it says "revised edition," you cite it as "rev. ed."

Number of volumes, if more than one.

Place of publication. Usually the name of the city is sufficient, though sometimes it's helpful to add a state or a country—"Cambridge," for instance, can be in England or in Massachusetts; there's a Newark in New Jersey and another in Delaware. With some books the list of places can go on forever: "London, New York, Toronto, Sydney, Christchurch, Johannesburg, New Delhi . . . ." That means only that the press has offices in many countries—the book was actually published in only one (or occasionally two) of them. In cases like this, it's usually safe to pick just the first one.

Name of the publisher. Use the name that appears on the title page, but omit things like "Incorporated" or "Ltd." Some guides recommend that you abbreviate "University Press" as "UP" or "Univ. Press"; others recommend you spell everything out. Just be consistent.

Year of publication. That's the year your particular edition was published, not the date of first publication—*Hamlet*, for instance, was first published in 1603, but you should cite the date of the edition you're using. There's no need to be any more precise than the year; Amazon.com may seem to give you the exact day of publication, but that information is often wrong, and it doesn't contribute anything anyhow. Stick with the year. Some people also like to indicate the year in which a title first appeared: you might, for instance, see something like "Daniel Defoe, *Robinson Crusoe*, ed. J. Donald Crowley (1719; Oxford: Oxford Univ. Press, 1972)." It means "first published in 1719, to help you put it in historical context, but the edition I'm using was published in 1972." That's optional.

When you cite *periodicals* (magazines, scholarly articles), provide the following:

The volume number of the journal. Most journals start a new volume each year, though they might not start in January—it's possible, for instance, to change volume numbers with the July issue.

The number (or issue number) of the journal, if it's published more often than annually. You can sometimes omit this, but only if the page numbers in the journal are continuous throughout the year—in other words, if number 2 picks up the page numbering where number 1 ended, and so on through the whole volume. If every issue begins with p. 1, then you have to include the issue number.

The date of publication. For annual journals, the year is plenty; for periodicals published more often, give the date as it appears on the title page of the journal: it might be just "2006"; it might be "Spring 2006"; it might be "May 2006"; it might be "21 May 2006." If you can omit the issue number (see above) you can give just the year; if you provide the issue number, give the full date.

The range of pages of the article in the periodical. In most cases this is a simple matter of giving the first and last page numbers. If an article is scattered throughout an issue—if, for instance, it begins on p. 132 and runs to p. 135, then there's a note "continues on p. 213," and it runs from there to p. 218, you'd give "pp. 132–35, 213–18" or something similar.

When you cite *newspapers*, provide the following:

The full name of the newspaper. Sometimes they name of the city or country of publication isn't in the title itself; in that case, if there's any danger of confusion, you can put the location in parentheses after the title—"*The New York Times*," but "*The Times* (Trenton)" or "*The Straits Times* (Singapore)."

The date of publication, to the day. In theory, newspapers have volume and issue numbers, but they're often hard to find, and they're sometimes not widely used.

The range of pages, if available. But note that some newspapers publish multiple editions each day, and an article may not be on the same page in every issue. In that case, you can omit the page references.

When you cite *Web sites*, provide the following:

Author and title, if they can be discerned. It's not always easy to tell, since many Web pages don't bother to provide the names (or at least the real names) of the creators, and many pages don't bear titles.

The URL of the page—that is, the Web address. This isn't always perfectly reliable: a URL might point to a page that contains multiple frames; it might not be persistent (i.e., it might work for only a single session, and not be usable tomorrow); it might be many lines long and nearly impossible for any mere mortal to type in. Still, a URL is the best we've got.

The date of the page, if it can be discerned. Things like on-line newspapers and blogs usually have pages of creation; many other pages include date of last revision.

The date of access—that is, when you read it. Since anything you cite today can change or even disappear tomorrow, it helps to let your audience know when you looked at it.

Notes and Bibliographies

There are two main places you can cite your sources: one is in notes (whether footnotes or endnotes); the other is in a list of works cited (sometimes called a bibliography).

If you're using notes, the usual rule is to provide a complete citation the first time you cite something—"Jane Smith, *A Sample Book* (New York: Knopf, 1993), p. 123"—and then to put subsequent citations in the text in an abbreviated form—"(Smith, p. 123)." There's no need for a separate bibliography, since you provide full details the first time you cite each work. Put the author's name in first-name-last-name order. *The Chicago Manual of Style* usually prefers this style of citation. (The *Chicago Manual* also allows for a "Works Cited" page, though it's less common to use Chicago style with a bibliography in the humanities.)

The rule for the works-cited approach is to put a brief citation of author and page in parentheses in the text—"(Smith 123)"—even on the first appearance, and then to have a separate bibliography (usually headed "Works Cited") at the end of the paper. Since your works cited are listed alphabetically by author, you list them by family name. The MLA favors this style. You can still use footnotes or endnotes, but they're for explanation or clarification, not for citation.

In a bibliography or works cited page, you list authors alphabetically by their family names. In English and many other languages, that involves reversing first and last names, which you do with a comma between last and first. There are a few exceptions:

> If a work has two or three authors, reverse the names only in the first one: "Smith, John, and Jane Doe"; "Smith, John, Jane Doe, and John Q. Public." If the list of authors gets longer than, say, three or four names, you can give just the first followed by "et al.," a Latin abbreviation for "and other [people]": "Smith, John, et al." Provide them in the order in which they appear on the title page.

Ancient writers (Homer, Virgil) usually go under a single name. (Roman writers had three names—Publius Vergilius Maro, Marcus Tullius Cicero—but in English we usually call them just "Virgil" or "Cicero.")

In the same vein, some medieval authors don't have last names, and go by their first, sometimes with a description. They're alphabetized by their given names: Bede (under B), Wolfram von Eschenbach (under W), Andreas Capellanus (under A). If you're unsure, ask someone or look at the copyright page of a book, a library catalogue, or an index to see how they're alphabetized there. See also the section on NAMES in the guide.

Some cultures don't put the personal name before the family name (as in some Hungarian, Korean, and Chinese names, where family name comes before personal name); in others, there is no family name, only a personal name (as in Icelandic, where a personal name is followed by a patronymic—the name of the father—so the singer Björk Guðmundsdóttir is alphabetized under B). If you don't reverse the order of the names, omit the comma.

Nobles are usually alphabetized under their titles: John Wilmot, the 2nd earl of Rochester, appears under "Rochester, John Wilmot, 2nd Earl of"; Henry St. John, Viscount Bolingbroke, appears under "Bolingbroke, Henry St. John, Viscount." This can get tricky when authors have multiple titles, changing over the years; even pros get confused on how to cite these. If you're stumped, check to see how your library catalogue gives the names.

Some works are anonymous: *Beowulf*, *La Chanson de Roland*, *Arden of Faversham*. In this case, omit the author's name and alphabetize the work by title.

CITING SPECIFIC PASSAGES

You usually have to cite specific passages in works, passages that appear on a single page or on a short range of pages. Providing page numbers is the normal way to do it. Some guides call for "p." before a single page number and "pp." for multiple pages; others leave out the "p." and give just the numbers—see the examples above. (Don't invent your own abbreviations: don't use *pg.* or *pgs.* or anything like that.)

When there's a range of pages you have to give the first and last page in the range. Both MLA and Chicago allow a few possibilities for page ranges. Suppose a passage begins on p. 123 and continues onto p. 124: do you cite it as "pp. 123–4," "pp. 123–24," or "pp. 123–124"? Different styles provide different guidelines. If you haven't received more specific guidelines, pick one style and be consistent.

Not everything, though, is quoted by page numbers:

> You usually cite poems by line number—or, for very long poems, book and line number (so, for instance, "*Odyssey*, 3.26–27"). This makes it easy to find passages even if the poem appears in different editions.

> With many plays, you cite act, scene, and line numbers. That's more common with older plays than with new ones. If the edition you're using includes act, scene, and line numbers, use them; if not, use page numbers.

> With some ancient Greek and Roman works, it's traditional to cite them with reference to other numbers that are uniform across all the editions and translations. The works of Plato, for instance, are usually cited by "Stephanus numbers," and Aristotle by "Becker numbers." You'll probably see them in the margins of the edition you're using. A few other authors are treated similarly.

> Reference books are usually cited by headword. If you want to quote the *Oxford English Dictionary*, for instance, you needn't spell out the volume and page numbers; ditto for encyclopedias. (It's understood that you found the information on the word *mulct* under the word *mulct*.) If, though, you discover something in a different entry from the obvious one—if, for instance, you find information about Einstein in the encyclopedia not under "Einstein, Albert," but in the general entry on "Physics"—you can use "s.v." (Latin *sub verbo*, "under the word") to indicate the source: "See *Encyclopædia Britannica*, s.v. 'Physics.'"

EXAMPLES

Here are some standard citation formats, as they appear in both Chicago and MLA. First comes a book, then a journal article, then a book article, and finally a Web page:

Books

Chicago (note)	MLA (works cited)
Tobias Smollett, *The Expedition of Humphry Clinker*, ed. Lewis M. Knapp (Oxford: Oxford Univ. Press, 1966).	Smollett, Tobias. *The Expedition of Humphry Clinker*. Ed. Lewis M. Knapp. Oxford: Oxford UP, 1966.

Articles in a Periodical

Chicago (note)	MLA (works cited)
Alan D. Hodder, "In the Glass of God's Word: Hooker's Pulpit Rhetoric and the Theater of Conversion," *New England Quarterly* 66, no. 1 (Spring 1993): 67–109.	Hodder, Alan D. "In the Glass of God's Word: Hooker's Pulpit Rhetoric and the Theater of Conversion." *New England Quarterly* 66.1 (1993): 67–109.

Articles or Chapters in a Book

Chicago (note)	MLA (works cited)
B. Hall, "Erasmus: Biblical Scholar and Reformer," in *Erasmus*, ed. T. A. Dorey (London: Routledge & Kegan Paul, 1970), pp. 81–113.	Hall, B. "Erasmus: Biblical Scholar and Reformer." *Erasmus*, ed. T. A. Dorey (London: Routledge & Kegan Paul, 1970). 81–113.

Web Sites

Chicago (note)	MLA (works cited)
Perry Willett, ed., *Victorian Women Writers Project*, http://www.indiana.edu/~letrs/vwwp/ (accessed 26 June 2002).	*Victorian Women Writers Project*. Ed. Perry Willett. May 2000. Indiana U. 26 June 2002 <http://www.indiana.edu/~letrs/vwwp/>.

PROBLEMS

There are plenty of difficult cases, and I can't explain them all here: they'd stretch to hundreds of pages. How, for instance, do you cite episodes of television programs?—government documents?—corporate annual reports?—interviews you conduct?—information gleaned in an on-line chat?—comments added to a blog posting? Standards for most of these are in the major style guides (Chicago and MLA), though the Internet presents a moving target for bibliographers. Most of the guides now provide citation styles for Web pages and such, but it's likely that technology will keep producing new forms of communication, and it sometimes takes years for them to make their way into the manuals.

When you're stumped and unable to find any appropriate guideline, don't fret too much. A good-faith effort to document the source of the information is usually enough. That will usually include the author's name (if it's known), the title of the work, the larger work of which it's a part, the date it appeared, and the publisher—whatever applies. And if you still can't figure out how to present a citation, talk to an instructor, a tutor at a writing center, or someone else who has good reason to know.

Additional Reading

There are countless writing guides, but many of them are awful. The books below are either classics in the field or my own faves.

H. W. Fowler, *Modern English Usage*. This seven-hundred-page volume of small type includes every conceivable stylistic point, arranged alphabetically, and written in an informal (but quirky) tone. Some of the entries are specific—several pages on punctuation—while others are general, such as tired clichés. Almost every entry has illustrative quotations from real life. Fowler was qualified for the job, having just compiled the *Concise Oxford Dictionary*. Yanks may find this classic work unsuitable because of its focus on British English, and much of it has been outdated in the eight decades since its first edition's completion. Still worth a look. A companion, *Modern American Usage* by Follett, makes up for some of Fowler's disadvantages, but lacks the charm of the original.

Sir Ernest Gowers *et al.*, *The Complete Plain Words*. Ernest Gowers's *Plain Words* is a guide to effective writing from the 1940s for British civil servants. Over the years it has gone through many editions and been changed by many hands. The most recent version, *The Complete Plain Words*, still shows its focus on British usage and the civil service, but many of its suggestions are excellent. Most of the book is a discussion of common writing problems, with examples of good and bad writing. There is also a long section on specific points of usage, arranged alphabetically.

George Orwell, "Politics and the English Language." Orwell's essay is one of the great works on the plain style. The essay should be available in any popular collection of Orwell's essays. Read it daily. Keep a copy under your pillow.

Thomas Pinney, *A Short Handbook and Style Sheet.* A handy little guide to style, written informally and accessibly. The general sections (on diction, vagueness, wordiness, and so on) are better than those devoted to mechanics. Pinney's work is refreshingly free of dogmatism of any sort.

Margaret Shertzer, *The Elements of Grammar.* Not bad if you're looking for very specific rules, but not highly recommended as a general guide. It includes things like "Capitalize nouns followed by a capitalized Roman numeral" and the proper spelling of *bête noire.* Easily available, since it's often sold with Strunk and White (below).

Strunk and White, *The Elements of Style.* The standard high school guide to style, and useful well beyond school. It includes a number of specific rules, dozens of commonly misused words, and bundles of suggestions for improving your style. Available anywhere (now including an on-line version of Strunk's 1918 edition). Read it. Memorize it. Live it.

Maxwell Nurnberg, *I Always Look Up the Word "Egregious": A Vocabulary Book for People Who Don't Need One.* A pleasant guide to building vocabulary that never becomes patronizing (the fault of too many books for beginners) or drifts off into utterly useless long words (the fault of too many books for fans of word games). It's probably too sophisticated for non-native speakers and rank beginners, but will help many others build a more powerful vocabulary.

The American Heritage Dictionary, 4th ed. Not only a good desk dictionary for providing definitions, but also a handy guide to usage on controversial questions. *AHD* has a panel of writers who vote on whether certain usages are acceptable.

Lynne Truss, *Eats, Shoots & Leaves: The Zero Tolerance Approach to Punctuation.* It's not a comprehensive treatise to answer all your questions, and it describes British rather than American practice. And the "zero-tolerance" stuff shouldn't be taken too seriously. But the book's a hoot, and if you're curious about the finer points of punctuation, check it out.